The New Life Challenge COOKBOOK

PATRICIA GILBERT, R.D., M.P.H., R.N.

REVIEW AND HERALD® PUBLISHING ASSOCIATION
Since 1861 | www.reviewandherald.com

Copyright © 2013 by Review and Herald® Publishing Association

Published by Review and Herald® Publishing Association, Hagerstown, MD 21741-1119

Cover design by Daniel Anez / Review and Herald® Design Center
Interior designed by the Review and Herald® Design Center

Photo credits:
  Joel D. Springer, photography / Tammie Bricker, food stylist: pages 3, 14, 17, 38, 42, 46, 50, 60, 65, 68, 74, 102, 114, 118

  © istockphoto.com pages 10, 18, 20, 22, 24, 26, 28, 30, 32, 36, 41, 44, 48, 54, 56, 58, 70, 72, 76, 78, 80, 82, 84, 86, 90, 92, 96, 98, 100, 106, 108, 110, 116, 124

  All other photos © Thinkstock.com

PRINTED IN U.S.A.

17 16 15 14 13   5 4 3 2 1

Library of Congress Cataloging-in-Publication Data
Gilbert, Patricia
        The New Life Challenge Cookbook, by Patricia Gillbert.
        1. Vegetarian cooking.   I. Title.

                                        641.5636

ISBN 978-0-8280-2710-6

The New Life Challenge

"The greatest challenge in life is to find a friend who knows all your flaws, differences, and mistakes, and yet still sees the best in you." — Unknown.

The authors of this book believe that all of us have aspirations to become better persons. Often it is the close friend or companion who helps to make life a little easier—the person who knows all about us but faithfully labors to help us see the best in ourselves. We have designed this cookbook to be a friend, so to speak.

Now we would like to introduce you to your new best friend—*The New Life Challenge Cookbook*. Your New Life Challenge friend knows that food is a necessity in life. With that in mind, we have created a cookbook that offers delicious and easy-to-make meals, but most important, it promotes a healthy lifestyle that will enable you to experience the wholeness you deserve—The New Life.

Like any good friend, this cookbook will encourage and coach you. It is said that real friends can never be mad at you for more than an hour, because they have something to tell you. So even when you slip up and overdo it, this cookbook just continues to share good life-activating recipes and compelling information to help you in your journey to better health for you and your family.

The New Life Challenge is more than a cookbook to place on the shelf, only to pull down whenever the occasional fad diet impulse hits. People have grown weary of starting and stopping such diets, only to become frustrated because of yet another failed attempt at weight loss. This cookbook will help you to arrive at The New Life you have longed for but found impossible to attain.

We invite you to take the challenge and receive The New Life. So whether you are looking to lose weight, overcome a lifestyle disease such as diabetes or high blood pressure, or perhaps become part of a growing trend to eat healthier foods but just haven't found recipes that work for you and your loved ones, this cookbook will assist you in your health goals, as well as let you reach the culinary standards your taste buds demand.

As you do so, you may take comfort in knowing that science and experience back up the principles of The New Life Challenge and this cookbook. With taste in mind, Pat Gilbert, our registered dietitian, has crafted these recipes.

—The New Life Challenge Team

The New Life

Apply these 10 principles in your life each and every day, and watch the difference it will make. Science has shown that each of them offers physiological health benefits.

Think of **THE NEW LIFE** as an acronym:

Trust More, Stress Less—Trust beyond yourself and limit stress

Have Refreshing Rest—Go to bed before 10:00 p.m.

Enjoy Sunshine—Get at least 15 minutes of sunlight at the healthiest hours of the day

Nutrition—Eat plant-based, nutrient-dense foods

Exercise—Walk, cycle, run, or swim, etc., at least 30 minutes a day

Water—Drink half your body weight in ounces of water or more

Live Temperately—Do *all* things in moderation, abstain from anything harmful, and limit that which is good

Invest Time in Others—Be thankful and serve others

Fresh Air—Breathe as much fresh air outdoors as you can

Educate Yourself—Constantly learn new life-sustaining knowledge for you and others

Each of these principles makes up The New Life. So, in essence, this cookbook is a teaching companion that helps you understand that diet is not the only key to health and happiness. However, much of it begins with diet and relates to all aspects of The New Life. For example, good nutrition is vital, but if you eat even good food just before bed, it will affect digestion so that you will receive no real benefit from the food and will not get any refreshing rest. Another example is that you could have the most nutritious meal, but if you sit at a computer all day and don't exercise, much of it will turn to fat, leading to extra weight.

Finally, we see that every aspect of The New Life has benefits. Sunlight helps with our body's need for vitamin D and good immune function. Fresh air and water not only improve blood circulation, but also help our brain perform its chemical processes. Stress lowers our immunity, so learning to manage it is critical. Throughout this book you will find principles of The New Life designed to help your body utilize the goodness of these dishes. Before long you will discover that health goes far beyond the kitchen table.

Principles, Diet, and a Boy Named Daniel

In order to understand the challenge, we turn to a famous story in which principles triumphed over challenging circumstances. The story of Daniel—most noted for being thrown into the lions' den—is one that actually began with an adherence to the principle of diet. Daniel lived a noble life in spite of extremely adverse circumstances. The historical records tell us of a Jewish captive who came to the ancient city of Babylon as just a teenager. Taken from his homeland in Jerusalem, he would spend the rest of his life in a foreign nation. Because he was young, healthy, and well, his captors chose him to serve in the king's palace.

Those whom the royal palace selected had to go through quite a bit of preparation, including learning a new language, having a name change, and accepting a new diet. For our purposes, we have focused our attention on the "new diet" aspect of the story. But in doing so, we discovered that it was Daniel's success on that point that led to his achievements in all other aspects of his life.

The king's official offered the young teenager food from the royal table. But it was food that Daniel had been trained not to eat. In other words, he understood the difference between clean and unclean foods. Daniel "purposed in his heart" (Daniel 1:8) not to defile his body with the king's food, and requested the Babylonian authorities to allow him to eat a simple, plant-based diet. As a result, he and his friends ate vegetables only for 10 days.

Soon Daniel was healthier than his peers: physically, mentally, and otherwise. This solid foundation was important in his future. He served under three despot monarchs, his companions were thrown into a burning furnace and lived to tell the story, and he himself wound up in a lions' den. Can you imagine the stress he should have been under? But history records that this noble young man became a composed and wise individual until his death.

It is important to note that the entire story of Daniel begins with a young man's choice in diet and a request to the king to allow him to live out the principles he knew and understood. Even in the midst of many challenges, he held to his convictions and experienced The New Life.

The Challenge

The New Life Challenge is a "wholeness" approach to reconditioning the entire person—mind, body, and spirit—for physical health, mental strength, personal discipline, and spiritual renewal. Their refusal to eat from the king's table was not a split-second decision for Daniel and his companions—it was a lifestyle choice, cultivated throughout their young lives. So The New Life Challenge is an opportunity to adopt a lifestyle change that mirrors the success of those Hebrew boys so long ago. Those young men understood a secret that is still important for us today. Let's think about human physiology for a moment. Blood is everything, and those young men knew it.

The Life of the Flesh Is in the Blood

Wait a minute! Are we discussing blood in a cookbook? Yes. When we consider that the body converts everything we eat to blood, we would be remiss if we did not share a basic concept that undergirds the foundation and purpose of these wonderful recipes.

Blood consists of trillions of cells. Everything in the body is made up of cells. As our blood flows through our circulatory system, delivering oxygen and nutrition, it repairs damage and removes waste. What we eat is important to how our body functions. We generate new skin cells every 28 days, new liver cells every five months, and new bone cells every 10 months. All of them get renewed or replaced using the foods we eat.

The organ that is our brain also consists of cells. In order for our brains to function well, we must have good, pure blood. Why? The brain needs oxygen, nutrition, and water to function properly. If it doesn't get sufficient blood, and therefore oxygen (as blood carries the oxygen), the results will be stroke or death. And if our blood circulation is poor, then our thoughts will also be sluggish. Good blood is necessary for clear thinking.

Eating and Digestion

We also need blood for good digestion. When we eat, blood rushes to the stomach to begin the very complex process of breaking food into the substances our bodies must have to live. All of this requires energy. The blood, to a large degree, supplies this energy. In short, if the body lacks good digestion, it will not experience good assimilation and absorption of the vitamins and minerals from the food that is necessary for good circulation of oxygen and nutrients to the brain.

So these young men had an understanding of how blood functions in the body because they were well aware of the ancient scrolls that stated, "the life of the flesh is in the blood" (Leviticus 17:11). They believed in the Levitical laws found in the Torah.

The New Life Challenge shares recipes that will help the body build good blood.

Good Science

True health is wholeness of the mind, body, and spirit. More than ever before, science tells us about the benefits of sunlight and water, and even the health benefits of doing good deeds. Many supporting studies for these principles have appeared in scientific journals in the past few years. One that is near and dear to The New Life Challenge team is a 2004 study by National Geographic and anthropologist and author Dan Buettner (*The Blue Zones*).

In 2004 Dan Buettner and National Geographic hired the world's best longevity researchers to identify pockets around the world where people lived measurably better—in fact, they lived so much better that they reached 100 years of age. In these Blue Zone pockets they found that people live to 100 or longer at rates 10 times greater than in the rest of the United States.

Such Blue Zones showed up in five very diverse areas and groups: Okinawa, Japan; Sardinia, Italy; Nicoya, Costa Rica; Icaria, Greece; and Loma Linda, California. As they studied these five groups more closely, they wanted to determine what they shared in common. Those traits included faith, family, and food, to name a few. Of course, the aspect we found most interesting was that food was a common denominator among all these 100-year-olds who were still exercising, driving themselves around, and enjoying life. The group in the Blue Zone in California adheres closely to the very same principles of The New Life.

The Loma Linda, California, group happened to be Seventh-day Adventists who typically eat a plant-based diet. They believe that human beings live best while following a diet derived from food nourished from the elements found in the dust of the ground, from which they also believe that God created humanity. It is interesting to note that according to the biblical account, when human beings began to eat animals their life span and longevity dropped significantly. What is even more fascinating about this is that this is exactly from where Daniel took the principles of his diet. It appears that he was following the same laws, the same principles.

A University of Memphis professor, Richard Bloomer, the interim chair of health sport sciences, recently replicated Daniel's dietary challenge. He is just the latest to conduct a study on Daniel's diet, providing evidence of its beneficial results even in the twenty-first century.

Bloomer and his research team's study consisted of 13 men and 30 women. Before the study began, researchers took their heart rate, blood pressure, and a blood sample. Subjects kept a record of the foods they consumed during a 21-day testing period. The results showed improvements in the risk factors for cardiovascular disease and metabolic diseases such as stroke and diabetes.

"We've seen weight loss, but the thing seen the most is a decrease in blood pressure, cholesterol, inflammation, and type 2 diabetics. Blood sugar levels decrease in as little as three weeks," Bloomer said.

We believe the key to optimal health is in understanding that there actually are laws of health. And nutrition is one of them. When followed, along with other healthy lifestyle choices, people can live above and beyond other people who eat contrary to such natural laws. Just as there are physical laws (such as the law of gravity) that have never failed, so, too, there are laws of health. They affect physical, mental, and even emotional health. The laws of nature govern seasons, rainstorms, plant growth, and even the human body. Whether we like it or not, the body must receive sunshine, water, good nutrition, fresh air, and all the other conditions of health that you will find in The New Life Challenge experience.

Motivated only by a desire for your total health, we urge you to embrace those essential health principles. As you enjoy the delectable meals presented in this cookbook, you will be challenged to learn, incorporate, and share those same principles. While results may vary based on current and past lifestyle patterns and family health history, within 10 weeks you should experience better health, peace of mind, and a more fulfilling existence. As you faithfully follow these principles, The New Life can be yours. We encourage your journey to The New Life with this cookbook . . . your new best friend. Let the journey begin.

Some Foods Listed in the Ingredients You May Be Unfamiliar With:

AGAR AGAR OR AGAR POWDER:
A vegetable gelatin made of a variety of sea vegetables with strong thickening properties. The seaweeds are boiled to a gel, pressed, dried, and crushed into flakes or powder. It will gel at room temperature. One brand is Eden Foods (www.edenfoods.com or found in whole food stores).

AGAVE NECTAR:
An all-natural nectar from the agave plant. It has a low glycemic index, which means it is slowly absorbed by the body and does not cause the same rapid increase in blood sugar as table sugar. It may be used in place of corn syrup in baking and cooking (www.honeytreehoney.com; this is found in most grocery stores where you would find honey).

BILL'S CHIK'NISH SEASONING:
Vegan, gluten-free, chicken-like seasoning. (www.billsbest.net, or whole food stores).

BRAGG'S LIQUID AMINOS:
All-purpose seasoning from soy protein. A soy sauce replacement that's lower in sodium. Gluten-free; unfermented (www.bragg.com; found in many grocery stores or whole food stores).

ENER-G BAKING POWDER:
Aluminum-free, sodium-free, gluten-free baking powder. The main ingredient is calcium carbonate. Using this baking powder in your foods will add calcium to your diet. You must substitute twice as much Ener-G baking powder to replace regular (sodium-based) baking powders. It does not work in all recipes. If you substitute sodium-based baking powder for Ener-G calcium-based baking powder, use half the amount (www.ener-g.com).

FLAXSEED AND FLAXSEED MEAL:
Flax-seeds are high in omega 3. They are also a great binding agent when flaxseed meal or flaxseed gel is mixed in foods. This is my favorite "egg" replacement in recipes. It can be found in the cereal section of grocery stores.

FLORIDA CRYSTALS:
Organic cane sugar. No bone char from animals are used in the filtering process that is prevalent in most sugar processing.

MCKAY'S CHICKEN- OR BEEF-STYLE INSTANT BROTH AND SEASONING:
No meat or meat by-products are used in their seasoning (www.mckays-seasoning.com; purchase in whole foods stores).

NUTRITIONAL YEAST FLAKES:
Ingredients are dried golden yeast flakes, and B vitamins. A tasty food supplement that can be sprinkled on popcorn or veggies or added to cheese sauces and tofu to give a cheesy flavor. This is not the same as the active yeast you use in baking bread. This is found in whole food stores.

MOZZARELLA VEGAN GOURMET:
This mozzarella cheese alternative is found in whole food stores (www.followyourheart.com).

TAHINI:
A creamy puree of roasted sesame seeds that has a light nutlike flavor. Also called sesame tahini. Tahini is high in calcium and found in most grocery and whole foods stores.

TEXTURED VEGETABLE PROTEIN UNFLAVORED CHUNK:
Found in whole foods stores. They are dehydrated so you need to hydrate them for 30+ minutes in Bragg's Liquid Aminos or another seasoning before adding them to recipes.

TOFU (WATER-PACKED AND SILKEN):
Tofu comes in soft to extra-firm consistencies. The extra-firm or firm holds together better than the soft when you cube it. The water-packed has a firmer texture; the silken tofu has a much creamier, silky texture. The silken tofu is preferable for smoothies and puddings. Mori-Nu Tofu is a boxed tofu that does not need to be refrigerated until opened.

Welcome to *The* New Life *Challenge*

This cookbook contains some of the most amazing recipes ever created. They are not only delicious but also healthy. In the following pages you will learn the simple steps to creating delicious recipes that will assist you in achieving better mental, physical, and spiritual health.

We believe that ancient Scripture has in its pages the answers for true happiness and that they are freely available to each one of us. In this cookbook you will find recipes that reinforce the 10 elements of The New Life Challenge. Not only are they based on scriptural principles—they are also backed up by countless scientific studies. For more information on the latest news and studies supporting the principles of The New Life Challenge, we invite you to check out our Web site at www.getthenewlife.com.

We have sought to keep it simple so that you can easily follow the steps of each recipe, and through our program we hope to show you why each element is a part of the big picture.

If you will take The New Life Challenge for 10 weeks and use this cookbook as you transition, we believe that you will feel better than you ever have before.

Table of Contents

Pumpkin Pie

Makes 8 Servings

Preheat Oven to 425°F

1 can (15 oz.)	pumpkin
½ cup	tofu white powder (or your favorite soymilk powder)
6 oz.	agave nectar
6 oz.	Silk soymilk
⅔ cup + 1 tbsp.	florida crystals
⅓ cup	all-purpose white flour
½ tsp.	ground cinnamon
¼ tsp.	ground ginger
¼ tsp.	ground nutmeg
½ tsp.	salt

Directions:

1 Mix agave nectar and tofu powder well and then add each of the other ingredients one at a time, mixing each well.

2 Pour into 9-inch unbaked pastry shell.

3 Bake at 425°F for 15 minutes. Reduce oven temp to 350°F and bake additional 40 minutes.

4 You may want to cover with foil while baking after 25 minutes to prevent it from getting brown on top.

NOTE:

To avoid any stomach irritation, try substituting cinnamon with coriander and nutmeg with cardamom.

NUTRITION

In the story of Daniel history records that after just 10 days on a plant-based diet, even his complexion improved.

Strawberry Pie

Makes 8 Servings
Preheat Oven to 375°F

Ingredients for Crust:

1½ cups	unbleached all-purpose flour
½ cup	wheat flour
¼ cup	toasted wheat germ
⅔ cup	florida crystals
⅔ cup	chopped pecans
⅔ cup	Earth Balance natural buttery spread (original), melted

Directions:

1 Combine dry ingredients in a bowl, pour in the melted buttery spread and mix with a fork until blended. Then press the mixture against a Pyrex pie plate.

2 Place piecrust in oven for 10 to 12 minutes. Check at 10 minutes and take out if lightly golden, otherwise bake 2 more minutes.

3 Take piecrust out of oven and cool. (You can make this a day ahead and keep cool in refrigerator until ready to use.)

NUTRITION

Desserts are lovely, tasty, and sweet, but you have promises to keep, and miles to go . . . don't overeat.

Ingredients for Cream Cheese Mixture to Smooth on Top of the Crust:

1 (8 oz.)	container Tofutti Better Than Cream Cheese
¼ cup + 2 tbsp.	florida crystals
2 (16 oz.)	containers of fresh ripe whole strawberries, washed and capped.

Directions:

1 Mix the cream cheese and sugar well, then smooth on the cooled piecrust with spatula.

2 Slice 1 cup of strawberries and set aside.

3 Place the capped whole fresh strawberries in the cream cheese piecrust with the capped end in the cream cheese and the tip of the strawberry pointing up.

Ingredients for Pie Filling:

1 cup	water
2 tbsp.	cornstarch
½ cup	florida crystals
1 cup	sliced fresh strawberries

Directions:

1 Heat water, cornstarch, and florida crystals in pan on stovetop until well dissolved; add sliced strawberries. Stir and *watch* as mixture thickens. Remove from heat. Cool.

2 Pour the strawberry filling over the whole strawberries. Refrigerate until ready to slice and eat. This pie is better if it is refrigerated for several hours before serving.

Mom's Cheesecake

Makes 8 Servings

Preheat Oven to 375° F

1 container	Tofutti Sour Supreme
2 containers	Tofutti Better Than Cream Cheese
1 tsp.	vanilla extract
¾ cup	florida crystals
2 tbsp.	all-purpose white flour

EDUCATE YOURSELF

Breast cancer rates are dramatically lower in nations that follow plant-based diets, such as China.

Directions:

1 Blend above ingredients in bowl with beater whips.

2 Pour into your favorite ready-made, extra-large graham cracker crust.

3 Bake at 375˚F for 20 minutes.

4 *Remove from oven and cool for 15 minutes. Then raise oven temp to 450˚F.*

5 Bake for 10 minutes more, then let cool.

6 Refrigerate overnight before serving.

7 Top with your favorite pie filling. Or I just make my own topping with fresh strawberries or blueberries. I also make a sweet gel with some of the berries, cornstarch, water, and florida crystals and heat on stovetop till translucent. Then cool, pour on top of the fresh fruit on the cheesecake, and return to refrigerator overnight before serving.

NOTE:

See Fruit Sauce Toppings recipes (p. 113).
This recipe was given to me by one of my students, Jerilyn, when I was teaching nutrition at a local university. It was her mother's recipe and is by far the best vegan cheesecake recipe I've ever eaten. No one believes it is truly vegan!

Fresh Blueberry Pie

Makes 8 Servings

1 quart	*Fresh* blueberries, washed and drained (this recipe will not work with frozen or canned berries)

Bring to Boil:

1 cup	blueberries
1 cup	florida crystals
½ cup	water

Once the mixture boils, make a smooth paste in a small bowl of:

⅓ cup	cold tap water
2½ tbsp.	cornstarch (mix well)

Directions:

1. Add this to the hot berries and stir until thickened. (It will not be very thick until it cools, then it will thicken up. I usually put the mixture in another bowl (to get it out of the hot pan) and put it in the refrigerator to cool.

2. When cool, add remaining berries (3 cups) to the thickened berries.

3. Pour into Nancy's wonderful piecrust (p. 19), and top with nondairy whipped topping.

4. Put in refrigerator about an hour to "set" and thicken, to be able to slice it nicely. This can be made a day ahead.

> It is not easy to put my progress in words, because it is beyond weight loss, smooth skin, better sleep, and so on. Yes I lost 20 pounds! What I am most thankful for is that the The New Life Challenge "agrees with me." Everything from the top of my head to my toes feels better and works better.
> —Shirlene Lewis-Gittens

Nancy's Wonderful 10-inch Piecrust

Makes 1 Piecrust
Preheat Oven to 400° F

Mix together in a bowl:

2 cups	unbleached all-purpose flour
½ cup	wheat germ
1 tsp.	salt
2 tsp.	florida crystals

Whisk together:

¾ cup	vegetable oil
¼ cup	soymilk

Directions:

1 Mix together wet and dry ingredients. I usually roll it out on a sheet of waxed paper and put another sheet of waxed paper on top.

2 Then I flip it into the pie pan. It may fall apart a little, but just press it together.

3 Bake until lightly browned (6 to 8 minutes). Cool. Then add filling. Refrigerate before slicing.

WATER

Water is needed for digestion. Drink plenty of water before your meals and avoid drinking with your meal.

Pecan Pie

Makes 8 Servings

Piecrust:

1 cup + 3 tbsp.	all-purpose flour
1 tbsp.	toasted wheat germ
½ cup	Earth Balance buttery spread
¼ cup	Tofutti Better Than Cream Cheese
½ tsp.	vanilla extract

Directions:

1 Mix together Earth Balance, cream cheese, and vanilla.

2 Stir in flour and wheat germ. Blend (with mixer or fingers), form into a ball, and place in the freezer for a few minutes.

3 Flour countertop and roll out the piecrust with rolling pin, dusting with flour to prevent sticking.

4 Put piecrust in pie pan, flute edges. Set aside.

NOTE:

Make sure you prick the piecrust bottom with a fork to prevent any air bubbles from making the crust rise and spilling the pie filling out of the pie.

Pie Filling:

¾ cup	flaxseed gel (see instructions below)
1 cup	agave nectar
1 cup + 1 tbsp.	florida crystals
2 tbsp.	flaxseed meal
¼ cup	chopped pecans
½ tbsp.	molasses
1 tsp.	vanilla extract
1 pinch	salt
1 tbsp.	agar agar powder
¼ cup	Earth Balance buttery spread
1 tbsp.	arrowroot flour/powder
1 cup	pecan halves

Directions:

1 Boil 3 tablespoons of flaxseeds in 1 cup water.

2 As soon as it begins to boil, pour the mixture through a fine mesh strainer into a stovetop pan to strain the seeds from the gel, and discard the seeds.

3 Add the following to flaxseed gel: agave nectar, florida crystals, flaxseed meal, chopped pecans, molasses, vanilla, salt, and agar agar powder.

4 In a separate bowl, mix together flour and margarine, then add to the syrup mixture, stirring well.

5 Continue to stir as mixture comes to a rapid full boil, then turn off heat and pour syrup mixture into uncooked piecrust.

6 Add pecan halves to top of pie, and bake for 35 minutes at 350°F.

7 Remove from oven and cool before slicing. Allow pie to thicken to room temperature. If you put the pie in the refrigerator, it will gel solid. Refrigerate leftovers; microwave leftover slices 15 to 20 seconds (see note below) to soften the pie filling if it is too stiff.

NOTE:

Do not microwave pie (to warm up) for more than a maximum of 25 seconds, or the pie will melt into syrup. One of my favorite ways to make pecan pie is to make pecan pie tarts. Use the same recipe, make 24 balls out of the dough. Shape the tiny dough crust in the Pam-sprayed tart pan. Pour in the pie filling, top with a pecan, and bake 25 to 30 minutes. These can be frozen and used later for a fast lunch box dessert or a quick elegant dessert.

Ice Cream

Peppermint Ice Cream

Makes 4 Servings

2 cups	Silk soymilk (plain)
⅔ cup	florida crystals
¼ tsp. + 3 drops	peppermint extract (flavoring is not as strong as extract)
¼ cup	crushed peppermints, set aside extra as a garnish

Directions:

1 Mix all ingredients together, except the extra crushed peppermint for garnish. Process in ice-cream maker until the ice cream has finished freezing.

2 Sprinkle extra crushed peppermint on top of each scoop as a garnish.

Strawberry Ice Cream

Makes 4 Servings

2 cups	Silk soymilk (plain)
⅔ cup	florida crystals
½ tsp.	strawberry flavoring
2 cups	capped strawberries divided (reserve 1 cup sliced for garnish)

Directions:

1 Process in the blender with light pulses. You want to leave visible strawberry pieces for texture and taste.

2 Process in ice-cream maker until the ice cream has finished freezing.

3 Serve with sliced strawberries on top.

Vanilla Ice Cream

Makes 4 Servings

2 cups	Silk soymilk (plain)
⅔ cup	florida crystals
1 tbsp.	vanilla extract

Directions:

1 Process until the ice cream is made.

2 Serve and enjoy.

NOTE:

All recipes for ice cream use Silk soymilk (plain), not vanilla flavored. For a creamier ice cream, use ½ cup Silk creamer (plain) and 1½ cup soymilk (plain). (Using more than ½ cup creamer does not freeze and will remain too soft.)

Pecan Pie Ice Cream

Makes 4 Servings

2 cups	Silk soymilk (plain)
⅓ cup	agave nectar
⅓ cup	florida crystals
¾ tsp.	molasses
½ tsp.	vanilla extract
1 tsp.	flaxseed meal
¼ cup	chopped pecans

Directions:

1 Whiz all the ingredients in the blender except chopped pecans.

2 Pour the mixture into the ice-cream maker, add chopped pecans, and process.

3 Serve with additional pecans sprinked on top.

EDUCATE YOURSELF

The dietary habits of 51,529 men, age 40 to 75, were examined to understand the relationship between prostate cancer and dietary fat. There was a clear correlation between an increased risk of advanced prostate cancer and the intake of animal fat, but not vegetable fat.

Wheat Berry "Meatballs" in Sweet and Sour Sauce

Makes 8 Servings

1 cup	wheat berries, plumped (marinated in ½ cup Bragg's—see directions below)
1 (12.3 oz.) box	Mori-nu Silken Tofu (firm), mashed
1 tube	Ritz crackers, crushed
1	onion, finely chopped
½ tsp.	sage
½ tsp.	salt
1 tbsp. + 1 tsp.	nutritional yeast flakes
2 tbsp.	flaxseed meal
3 tbsp.	gluten flour
1½ tsp.	garlic powder

Directions:

1. 1 cup wheat berries plumped overnight in water. Drain the water off the wheat berries the next day. Add ½ cup Bragg's Liquid Aminos (or soy sauce) and marinate a minimum of 20 minutes.

2. Drain Bragg's Liquid Aminos off wheat berries and set liquid aside to use in Sweet and Sour Sauce. Place wheat berries in a food processor until broken into small pieces. Transfer to a bowl. Add the remaining ingredients together and mix well. You may need to add a little Bragg's Liquid Aminos if the mixture is too dry to form into balls. Pinch off and roll into balls or make patties.

3. Bake at 350°F for 45 minutes. These freeze well.

Sweet and Sour Sauce
Makes 8 Servings

1 cup	brown sugar
1½ cup	ketchup
¼ cup	barbeque sauce
1 tsp.	Bragg's Liquid Aminos
½ tsp.	lemon juice
¾ cup	water

Directions:

1. Mix above ingredients together, then cover the cooked "meatballs."

2. Bake at 350°F for 30 minutes. Serve with mixed vegetables and potato or rice.

Prime Rolls

Makes 6 Servings

Filling:

1 (16 oz.) can	drained pinto beans
1 cup	Loma Linda canned Vege-Burger
1 medium	onion, chopped
1 medium	bell pepper, chopped
2 cloves	garlic, minced
1 tsp.	McKay's Beef-Style Seasoning
1 tsp.	Bragg's Liquid Aminos or soy sauce
½ tsp.	onion salt
½ tsp.	garlic salt

Directions:

1 Sauté onion, bell pepper, and garlic in water until soft and translucent. Drain.

2 Add drained pinto beans. Mash beans to a paste.

3 Add Vege-Burger, beef-style seasoning, Bragg's Liquid Aminos, onion salt, and garlic salt.

4 Stir well and heat on medium-high until steaming. Turn heat off. Set mixture aside.

Rolls:

1½ cups	soymilk (plain), hot
1 cup	rolled old-fashioned oats
1 tsp.	salt
¼ cup	canola oil
2 tbsp.	florida crystals
2 tbsp.	yeast
2 cups	all-purpose flour
¼ cup	whole-wheat flour
¼ cup	toasted wheat germ

Directions:

1 Add oats, salt, oil, and florida crystals to hot soymilk.

2 When soymilk cools down to warm temperature, add yeast. When mixture starts to foam and bubble, add flour and wheat germ.

3 Stir and make soft dough (you do not need to knead this dough). Turn out dough onto a floured surface (you may need to add more flour to achieve the right consistency). Roll out a 10" x 13" rectangle.

4 Spoon bean paste mixture onto dough and smooth out to edges of dough.

5 Roll dough lengthwise. Cut into 1-inch sections. Place on cookie sheet; do not let them touch.

6 Bake at 350°F for 30 minutes or until toothpick inserted into the dough comes out clean.

7 Serve with gravy. (Baked butternut squash or yellow squash with onions, mashed potatoes, and salad complement this meal.)

NOTE:

Cutting the Prime Rolls is easier if you use sewing thread or unwaxed dental floss: put the thread under the end of the roll; bring both ends of thread up on each side of roll and pull across the roll.

Prime Rolls freeze well. Warm them up and top with gravy.

Asian Curried Vegetables With Tofu

Makes 4 Servings

4 to 5 cups   cooked brown rice (set aside)

Tofu step 1: Drying

1½ cups (24 oz.) water-packed extra-firm tofu

Directions:

1. Remove tofu from container and wrap in a towel or several paper towels. Set in a large bowl and put a weighted container on it for 15 to 30 minutes (removing excess water from tofu allows it to absorb better).
2. While the tofu is wrapped, make the marinade.

Marinade:

2 cups	water
2 tbsp.	Bragg's Liquid Aminos
2 tsp.	McKay's Chicken-Style Seasoning
1 tsp.	garlic powder
⅛ tsp.	curry

Directions:

Mix together the above ingredients and set aside.

Tofu step 2: Marinating

Directions:

1. Remove the weight and unwrap the tofu from the towel.
2. Cut tofu into ¼-inch by 1½-inch rectangles.
3. Add the rectangular tofu to marinade and let marinate in refrigerator at least 4 hours or overnight.

Tofu step 3: Coating

1. Place 1-2 cups Panko Japanese Bread Flakes or crumbs in a separate bowl.
2. Stir in 4 tablespoons nutritional yeast flakes into Panko flakes.
3. Remove tofu from marinade, bread with Panko flakes and nutritional yeast flakes. Set aside.

Tofu step 4: Frying (need canola oil)

Directions:

1. Fry breaded tofu in small quantities of canola oil.
2. The oil should be medium-high heat and *hot* before you put the tofu into the oil. The tofu should immediately start frying when placed in the oil.
3. Watch carefully and turn to make sure all sides are cooked equally.
4. You will need to add more oil to the pan while frying batches of breaded tofu.
5. Transfer fried tofu to a plate lined with paper towels to soak up any excess oil.

Vegetables:

1	onion, chopped
½ cup	bell pepper, chopped
1 stalk	celery, chopped
2	carrots, chopped
1 tsp.	garlic salt
¾ tsp.	curry (or to taste)
½ tsp.	salt
	water

Directions:

1. Sauté onion, bell pepper, celery, and carrots in enough water to cover and cook until tender and water is evaporated.
2. Stir in cooked rice, salt, garlic salt, and curry. Cook on medium-high heat until steaming.
3. Place curry rice and vegetables on serving plate or bowl, add tofu to the top.
4. Complete the meal with a tossed salad.

NOTE:
For oil-free, bake tofu at 350°F for 15 to 20 minutes on a cookie sheet.

General Tso's Tofu

Makes 4 Servings

several crowns	broccoli, cut, ready to steam, enough for 4 to 5 people
2½ cups	brown rice + 5 cups water put into rice maker.
1½ cups (24 oz.) water-packed extra-firm tofu	

Step 1: Drying

Directions:

1. Remove tofu from container and wrap each one in a kitchen towel.
2. Set in a large bowl and put a weighted container on it for 15 to 30 minutes (removing excess water from tofu allows it to absorb better).
3. While the tofu is wrapped make the marinade.

Marinade:

¾ cup	Bragg's Liquid Aminos
2½ tbsp.	General Tso Sauce (Iron Chef or your favorite brand)
1½ cups	water
2 tbsp.	grated fresh ginger
2 tbsp.	agave nectar
2 tbsp.	minced fresh garlic
2 tbsp.	sesame oil (optional)
½ tsp.	sambal oelek ground fresh chili paste (may increase)

Directions:

1. Mix together the marinade ingredients.
2. Set aside.

Step 2: Marinating

1. Remove the weight and unwrap the tofu from the towel.
2. Cut tofu into 1-inch cubes.
3. Add the cubed tofu to the marinade, cover and let marinate in refrigerator at least 4 hours, or overnight. Marinating the night before serving this entrée makes the tofu taste much better and is less work on the day it is served.

(continued on page 34)

> I dropped 15 pounds, and the weight is still dropping. I would absolutely recommend this to anyone.
> —Dick Knipple

Step 3: Coating

1+ cup   cornstarch

Directions:

1 Remove tofu cubes from the marinade, drain in colander, and set in bowl.

2 Set marinade aside to be used later as a sauce.

3 Gently toss tofu cubes in 1+ cup cornstarch. Make sure that each side gets thoroughly coated and no moisture is present on the tofu. Set tofu aside until ready to fry.

NOTE:

Save the excess cornstarch to be used later in this recipe.

You will want to start steaming the broccoli when you have almost finished frying the tofu.

> When I took The New Life Challenge, I had serious problems with poor circulation and was on the verge of amputation of my lower right leg. I was given my life back through this wonderful program.
> I lost 33 pounds, started feeling good physically, sharp mentally, and a deep fulfillment in my soul. Most of all I now have tools to help others.
> —Anna K. Taylor

Step 4: Frying (need canola oil)

Directions:

1 Fry the cornstarch-covered tofu in small quantities of canola oil.

2 The oil should be on medium-high heat and *hot* before you put the tofu into the oil. The tofu should immediately start frying when placed in the oil.

3 Watch carefully and turn to make sure all sides are cooked equally.

4 You will need to add more oil to the pan while frying batches of cornstarch-covered tofu.

5 Transfer fried tofu to a plate lined with paper towels to soak up any excess oil until frying has been completed.

6 Finished tofu cubes should be crispy and slightly browned on the outside and soft on the inside.

7 Take the hot frying pan and pour out excess oil.

8 Take approximately 1 to 2 tablespoons of the excess cornstarch you used to coat the tofu and mix it in the marinade. Put the marinade in the frying pan and bring to a boil. Add 1 tablespoon + 1 teaspoon florida crystals. Turn off heat and set aside.

9 Place cooked rice on a platter. Arrange steamed broccoli around the outside of the rice. Drizzle half of marinade over the rice. Use the other half of marinade in a serving bowl for extra helpings at the table. Place tofu on top of marinade-covered rice.

10 Garnish with 2 chopped scallions and 2 tablespoons to ¼ cup sesame seeds.

NOTE:

For oil-free, bake marinated tofu in the oven at 350°F for 15 to 20 minutes on a cookie sheet.

Another way to use less oil in frying is to spray a nonstick skillet with Pam and heat to medium-high. Spray Pam on the coated tofu and place in skillet to fry. Turn tofu cubes, spray with Pam again, continue to fry.

Turn and spray with Pam until all sides are brown.

Thai Red Curry Paste

Makes 1 Cup

1.5 oz.	sambal oelek ground fresh chili paste
3 tbsp.	peanut butter
⅓ cup	heaping chopped green onions
¼ cup	peeled whole garlic cloves
5-6 drops	lime juice
2½ tbsp.	peeled, chopped, fresh ginger
¾ tsp.	whole coriander seed or powder

Directions:

1 Dry-roast the coriander seed in a small skillet over medium heat for 4 minutes or until toasted. (Disregard if you have coriander powder). Transfer to a bowl and set aside to cool.

2 Put green onions and garlic in skillet and dry-roast over medium heat until tender; stir often.

3 Remove from skillet and set aside to cool.

4 Put roasted coriander seed in mortar and grind to a powder.

5 Put coriander powder in food processor with metal blade.

6 Pound ginger in mortar, then transfer to food processor.

7 Transfer garlic, onions, peanut butter, lime juice, and chili paste to food processor.

8 Process until moist paste forms.

NOTE:

This paste can be stored in an airtight container in the refrigerator for 1 month, or in freezer for up to 3 months. Once the paste is made, it can be divided into tablespoon portions. Place the portions on wax paper to freeze. Then place in a labeled ziplock bag for future use.

WATER

Liquid dilutes your digestive juices, leading to improper digestion.

Thai Cashew Tofu

Makes 4 Servings

4-5 cups	cooked brown rice
½ cup	roasted cashews for garnish
1½ cups (24 oz.)	water-packed extra-firm tofu

Tofu step 1: Drying

Directions:

1 Remove tofu from container and wrap in a towel.

2 Set in a large bowl and put a weighted container on it for 15 to 30 minutes (removing excess water from tofu allows it to absorb better).

3 While the tofu is wrapped, make the marinade.

Marinade for Tofu:

2 cups	water
2 tbsp.	Bragg's Liquid Aminos
2 tsp.	McKay's Chicken-Style Seasoning
½ tsp.	garlic powder

Directions:

Mix together the above ingredients of marinade and set aside.

Tofu step 2: Marinating

Directions:

1 Remove the weight and unwrap the tofu from the towel.

2 Cut tofu into ½-inch cubes.

3 Add the tofu to marinade and let marinate in refrigerator at least 4 hours or overnight.

Tofu step 3: Coating

Directions:

1 Place 1-2 cups Panko Japanese Bread Crumbs in a bowl.

2 Stir in 3 tablespoons nutritional yeast flakes.

3 Remove tofu from marinade, discard the marinate.

4 Bread tofu with Panko flakes and nutritional yeast flakes. Set aside.

Tofu step 4: Frying (need canola oil)

Directions:

1 Fry breaded tofu in small quantities of canola oil.

2 The oil should be on medium-high heat and *hot* before you put the tofu into the oil. The tofu should immediately start frying when placed in the oil.

3 Watch carefully and turn to make sure all sides are cooked equally.

4 You will need to add more oil to the pan while frying batches of tofu.

5 Transfer fried tofu to a plate lined with paper towels to soak up any excess oil.

NOTE:
For oil-free, bake breaded tofu at 350°F for 15 to 20 minutes on a cookie sheet.

Thai Cashew Sauce:

2 tsp.	Thai Red Curry Paste (p. 35)
2 cups	water, with
2 tsp.	Bill's Best Chick'Nish seasoning
¼ cup	florida crystals
¼ cup	Bragg's Liquid Aminos
2 tbsp.	cornstarch
½ cup	roasted cashews

Directions:

Mix together the above ingredients in a skillet on medium heat until bubbling, then reduce to simmer.

Vegetables for Thai Cashew Tofu:

1 cup	snow peas (can substitute green beans cut lengthwise)
1	onion, chopped in narrow slices
1	bell pepper, chopped in narrow slices
4	spring onions, chopped, including green tops
6+	shitake mushrooms, sliced (optional)

Directions:

1 Sauté above veggies in water until soft and liquid has evaporated.

2 Pour Thai Cashew Sauce (see above) on the vegetables in skillet on medium-high heat and mix. Turn off heat. Ladle cashew sauce with vegetables on top of cooked rice.

3 Place breaded tofu on top.

4 Garnish with roasted cashews.

5 Serve with Thai Salad and Thai Curried Peanut Salad Dressing (both on page 39).

Thai Curried Peanut Salad Dressing

Makes 6 Servings

¾ cup	light coconut milk
½ tbsp.	curry paste (p. 35)
½ cup	water
¼ tsp.	Bill's Best Chick'Nish seasoning or similar
½ cup	chunky peanut butter
3 tbsp.	florida crystals

Directions:

1 Pour coconut milk in pan and start cooking on medium-high heat.

2 Stir in curry paste, and bring to a boil. Turn down heat to medium, stirring constantly.

3 Add water and Chik'Nish seasoning.

4 Reduce heat to low, stir in peanut butter, cook for 2 minutes.

5 Add florida crystals and cook until dissolved.

6 Cool and keep in refrigerator until ready to serve.

> I am 71 years old and have lost nearly 20 pounds now. I am also no longer on my blood pressure medication. I live around people right now who have so many health issues, and I would like to be there to answer their questions.
> —Mary Bond

Thai Salad

Makes 4 Servings

	red leaf lettuce, chopped
1	cucumber, sliced
1	carrot, shredded
2	scallions, chopped
¼ cup	red cabbage, shredded

Directions:

Toss together and serve with Thai Curried Peanut Salad Dressing on the side.

NOTE:

A lower fat option—substitute coconut milk with ¾ cup almond milk or Silk soymilk mixed with ¼ teaspoon coconut extract plus 1 teaspoon cornstarch or 1 teaspoon flour. Mix well before adding to the recipe.

Panang Tofu Curry

Makes 4 Servings

4 to 5 cups	cooked brown rice
1 pkg. (16 oz.)	water-packed tofu extra-firm, drained, wrapped in a towel, and set in bowl with something heavy on it to get the liquid out. Then cut into small cubes (¼-inch cubes). Set aside.
1 cup	carrots, sliced
½ cup	sweet potatoes, cubed
½ cup	spring onions, chopped (save 2 tbsp. for garnish)
4	garlic cloves, minced
½ cup	onion, chopped
½ cup	red or green bell pepper
1 cup	water, combined with
1 tsp.	Bill's Best Chick'Nish seasoning
1 (13 to 14 oz.)	can light coconut milk
1½ tsp.	Thai Red Curry Paste (p. 35)
¼ cup	chunky peanut butter
¼ cup	fresh cilantro
1 tsp.	turmeric
½ tsp.	cumin
1¼ tsp.	salt
¼ tsp.	lime juice
1 tbsp.	ketchup
2 tbsp.	florida crystals
2 tbsp.	Bragg's Liquid Aminos
	chopped peanuts for garnish

Directions:

1 Put carrots and sweet potatoes in enough water to cover and cook until tender. Set aside. Put spring onions, garlic, onion, and bell pepper in enough water to cover and cook until tender.

2 Add carrots and sweet potatoes to cooked onion mixture.

3 Add water with Chik'Nish seasoning, coconut milk, curry paste, peanut butter, fresh cilantro, turmeric, cumin, salt, lime juice, ketchup, florida crystals, and Bragg's Liquid Aminos.

4 Bring to medium heat and stir. After it begins to steam, cover and turn down heat.

5 Add tofu cubes and simmer for 30 minutes to let the tofu absorb the flavors. (This can be put in the refrigerator and served the next day, just heat up.)

6 To serve, place hot rice on plate and top with Panang Tofu Curry.

7 Garnish with 2 tablespoons chopped spring onions and sprinkling of chopped peanuts.

NOTE:

A lower fat option—substitute coconut milk with 1 3-ounce almond milk or Silk soymilk mixed with ½ teaspoon coconut extract plus 1 tablespoon cornstarch or 1 tablespoon flour. Mix well before adding to the curry recipe.

Spinach Tomato Quiche

Makes 8 Servings
Preheat Oven to 350°F

Piecrust:

1 cup	all-purpose unbleached flour
2 tbsp.	toasted wheat germ
¼ cup + 2 tbsp.	Earth Balance buttery spread
¼ tsp.	salt
¼ cup	cold water

Directions:

Combine flour, wheat germ, Earth Balance, and salt in food processor until mixed. Add cold water and process again. Remove and form into a ball, then roll out on floured surface. Place in pie plate. Set aside.

Filling:

1½ cups	Deb's Notso Cheeze (p. 47)
4 oz.	Better Than Cream Cheese (plain)
½ pkg.	water-packed firm tofu, drained, wrapped in a towel, with heavy weight on it to soak up the extra water, then crumbled
½ pkg. (5 oz.)	vegan gourmet mozzarella cheese, shredded, set aside to sprinkle on top of quiche before baking.
1 medium	white potato microwaved until done, then peeled and chopped
½	chopped onion, sautéed in water until soft, drained
3 cups	fresh spinach, cooked, drained, squeezed to get extra water out, cut
½ cup	flaxseed meal
½ cup	all-purpose unbleached flour
1 tbsp.	nutritional yeast flakes
1½ tsp.	onion salt
1 tsp.	salt
1 cup	fresh tomatoes, chopped

Directions:

1 Transfer 1½ cups of Deb's Notso Cheeze to a large bowl, add cream cheese, and mix together well.

2 Add crumbled tofu, chopped potato, onion, spinach, flaxseed meal, flour, nutritional yeast, onion salt, salt, and drained tomatoes, and pour into piecrust.

3 Bake 40 minutes. Remove from the oven and sprinkle shredded vegan cheese on top of the quiche. Turn oven temperature to broil for 3 to 5 minutes to melt the vegan cheese. *Set timer* as it will burn if not closely watched.

4 Allow to cool for a few minutes before cutting.

5 Serve with steamed kale and baked acorn squash or corn on the cob.

NOTE:

The Vegan Gourmet Cheese Alternative Mozzarella is an optional ingredient simply for presentation. It has melted appealing look. But it tastes great without the cheese topping.

Ratatouille on Quinoa

Makes 8 Servings

1	eggplant, peeled, cut into ¼-inch chunks
1	onion, chopped
1	bell pepper, chopped
1	zucchini, sliced
1	yellow squash, sliced
½ cup	mushrooms, sliced (optional)
2-3	garlic cloves, minced
3	fresh basil leaves, snipped to small pieces
1 tsp.	Bill's Best Chick'Nish seasoning
1 tsp.	garlic salt
¼ tsp.	oregano
1 can	garbanzos, drained
1 jar (24 oz.)	spaghetti sauce
1½ cups	quinoa (dry)

EXERCISE

Take a brisk walk after this recipe, which will aid in digestion.

Directions:

1 Place quinoa in a rice maker and add 3¼ cups water, cook.

2 Steam eggplant chunks until soft. Sauté the following in water until soft: onion, bell pepper, zucchini, squash, mushrooms, and garlic. Add enough water in the pan to keep the veggies from sticking and burning. When the veggies are soft, add basil, Chik'Nish seasoning, garlic salt, oregano, garbanzos, and spaghetti sauce and turn heat to medium until bubbling. Then turn heat down to simmer until ready to serve on quinoa.

3 Add a salad and french bread for a hearty meal.

Mexican Salsa

Makes 4 Cups (Serves 8+)

1	onion, quartered
1	bell pepper, quartered (remove inside seeds)
1	banana pepper (remove inside seeds)
½ -⅓ bunch	cilantro (depending on your taste)
1 tsp.	salt
1 tbsp.	lime juice
2 cans (14.5 oz.)	tomatoes, peeled, diced

Directions:

Combine ingredients in a food processor and pulse until you get the consistency you desire.

NOTE:

To kick up the heat add jalapeno or fresno pepper. For extreme heat add cayenne pepper. (Use gloves when handling.) Removing seeds helps decrease the heat.

Deb's Notso Cheeze

Makes 4+ Cups

3 cups	cold water
2 cups	raw cashews (can use roasted)
2 tbsp.	tahini (roasted and pureed sesame seeds)
2 tbsp.	nutritional yeast flakes (sold at health food store)
1 tbsp.	salt
1½ tsp.	onion powder
2 tbsp.	whole-wheat flour
½	fresh red pepper (or 2-oz. jar of pimiento)
1 tsp.	lemon juice concentrate or juice from 1 fresh lemon

Directions:

1. Blend until smooth.
2. Warm over medium heat until thickened, about 20 to 30 minutes, stirring often.

NOTE:

Add RoTel original diced tomatoes and green chilies to your taste for a hot cheesy Mexican dip. Start with ½ can; add more to heat it up!

This cheese freezes well. It has the very same consistency when thawed from the freezer.

INVEST TIME IN OTHERS

Make enough of each of these recipes to share with a neighbor, friend, or colleague.

Tostada Del Mondo or Burrito

Makes 4 Servings

1 pkg.	10-inch flour tortillas
¼ cup	Earth Balance natural buttery spread
1 can	pinto or black beans, well drained
¼ tsp.	cumin
⅓ cup	water
2	garlic cloves, minced
½ cup	onion, chopped, set aside half for garnishing
	shredded lettuce
1-2	tomatoes, chopped
	black olives, sliced
	Tofutti Better Than Sour Cream
	Deb's Notso Cheeze
	Mexican Salsa
	avocado, sliced (optional)
2	scallions, chopped, including tops

Tostada Directions:

1 Sauté garlic and onion in water until soft, add cumin and beans. When beans begin to bubble, take a potato masher and mash sufficiently until it looks like refried beans. Turn heat to low.

2 Lightly cover both sides of flour tortilla with small amount of Earth Balance. Fry 4 tortillas on both sides in a nonstick skillet.

3 Take one fried tortilla, spread ¼ of the bean mixture on the tortilla, spread Deb's Notso Cheeze on top of the beans, place lettuce on top of cheese, followed by tomato, olives, sour cream, salsa, avocado, and scallions.

Burrito Directions:

Sauté garlic and onion in water until soft; add cumin and beans. Mash beans. Warm the tortilla in microwave on plate for 15 seconds. Remove. Smooth Deb's Notso Cheeze on total surface of tortilla. Put spoonfuls of beans down center of tortilla; add sour cream, lettuce, tomato, olives, salsa, and avocado. Fold up burrito. Top with Deb's Notso Cheeze and scallions.

NOTE:

You may use Mexican Rice (p. 53) as a side dish or add it to the layering.

EDUCATE YOURSELF

A diet high in protein from an animal source can lead to osteoporosis. Vegetarians are at a lower risk for osteoporosis. Since animal products force calcium out of the body, eating meat can promote bone loss. In nations with mainly vegetable diets (and without dairy product consumption), osteoporosis is less common than in the U.S., even when calicum intake is also less than in the U.S.

Enchiladas

Makes 5 Servings

NOTE:
10 soft flour tortillas and items listed below for sauce and filling. For garnish: extra sour cream, avocado, and fresh chopped chives and cilantro.

Sauce

1 can (28 oz.)	peeled tomatoes blended in blender

Directions:

Place in large saucepan on stove with medium heat and add:

1	small onion, chopped
1	small green pepper, chopped
½ tsp.	garlic powder
½ tsp.	salt
⅛ tsp.	celery seed

Directions:

1 Cook above ingredients until onion and pepper are soft.

2 In a separate bowl, mix 1 heaping tablespoon flour with 1 tablespoon melted margarine. Mix that into the tomato mixture.

3 Add ½ cup Tofutti Sour Cream into the tomato mixture and stir until it thickens, then turn off heat and set it aside.

Enchilada:

Mix the following together and set aside.

1 large can	drained pinto or black beans (2 lb. 8½ oz. family size), mashed
¼ cup	salsa (your favorite, mild, medium, or hot; can also add green chilies for hotter taste buds)
½ tsp.	garlic powder

To put the enchilada together:

1 Take flour tortillas and set beside the sauce mixture. Dip tortilla into tomato sauce mixture. Remove from tomato sauce. Spoon bean mixture into center of the tortilla. Roll up tortilla, leave the ends open and place seam side down in the Pam-sprayed casserole dish. Repeat with the remaining tortillas. Place close together in casserole.

2 Pour the remainder of the sauce over the rolled up tortillas. Bake at 375°F for 20 minutes uncovered.

3 Garnish with sour cream, sliced avocado, and fresh chopped chives and cilantro.

NUTRITION

Good fats will suppress hunger longer, while giving you more energy throughout the day. Add a handful of nuts or avacado to your salad.

Mexican Rice

Makes 6-8 Servings

3 cups	brown rice
1 can (6 oz.)	tomato paste, mixed well with
1 cup	water
1 cup	frozen mixed vegetables
½ cup	salsa
1½ tsp.	salt
1 tsp.	garlic salt
1 tsp.	garlic powder
½	onion, chopped
2	garlic cloves, minced
5 cups	water

Directions:

Put all ingredients in a rice cooker (total liquid is 6 cups). Stir before turning on cooker.

NOTE:

Watch carefully and stir a few times near the end of cooking so the rice does not stick to the bottom of the rice cooker and burn.

NUTRITION

Looks like the old wives' tale of not swimming after you eat. Well, it's true. Blood is needed for digestion in the stomach, but goes to the extremities, impeding good digestion.

Rolled Tacos

Makes 6 Servings

(for dipping in salsa and cheese)

	flour tortillas
1 can	pinto or black beans cooked and mashed (to make refried beans)
	Deb's Notso Cheeze
¼ cup	vegetable oil

Directions:

1 Spread tortillas with light layer of refried beans and "cheeze," then roll up tightly. Or you can just spread with Deb's Notso Cheeze

2 Fry in oil. Place on plate with paper towel to absorb excess oil.

3 Serve with Mexican Salsa, and/or Deb's Notso Cheeze with RoTel (warm on stovetop or microwave before serving for a hot cheesy Mexican dip).

NOTE:

For a lower fat option: Spray frying pan with Pam, fry rolled tacos (turning often) until they are lightly browned. You may need to reapply with Pam between tacos.

Potato Gnocchi

Makes 6 Servings

2	medium baking potatoes
½ cup	all-purpose flour
1 tsp.	salt
¼ tsp.	garlic powder
¼ tsp.	onion powder
⅛ tsp.	basil

Directions:

1 Pierce each potato with a knife. Cook the potatoes in a microwave until soft.

2 Place flour and seasoning in a bowl and mix well. Set aside.

3 Remove potatoes from the microwave. Allow them to cool enough to handle. Remove the skin from one potato.

4 Push 1 potato though a potato ricer. If you do not have a potato ricer, mash the potato through a small wire mesh strainer by pushing the potato through the mesh with the back of a spoon. Let the strained potato fall into the flour. Repeat with the second potato. It's these fine pieces of potato that make this recipe work.

5 Lightly mix the flour and potato with a fork until well blended.

6 Form dough with your hands, making a ball.

7 Divide the dough into 4 equal balls.

8 Shape each ball into an 18-inch rope of dough. Cut the rope into 1-inch pieces.

9 With the back of a fork, press a 1-inch "pillow" of dough up against the fork to leave the characteristic ridges on one side and an indention on the other.

10 Place the small "pillows" in a bowl and lightly dust with flour, to keep the gnocchi separated.

11 Store in a covered container in freezer until ready to boil.

12 Heat water to a slow boil.

13 Drop gnocchi into water; it will rise when done (2 minutes). Ladle to a colander and drain.

14 Cook gnocchi in small batches.

15 Combine gnocchi with garlic cream sauce, pesto sauce, marinara sauce, or a mixture of olive oil, Italian seasoning, and Vegan Parmesan Cheese (p. 125).

16 Store leftovers flat on wax paper, refrigerate, then freeze in labeled ziplock bags for later use.

NOTE:

If too dry to roll out into ropes, add water to your hands when rolling out onto a surface. If too wet, add a small amount of flour.

This recipe will work only with microwaved potatoes or potatoes baked uncovered. The skin of the potato must be dry, as opposed to a "wet" steamed potato.

Do not use more flour except to roll out into ropes or to keep the pillows separated, or you will get dumplings instead of potato gnocchi.

Gnocchi Variations:

Sweet Potato Gnocchi Directions:

Use 1 sweet potato and 1 baking potato as it will hold together better. (Follow the previous directions for seasonings, etc.)

Spinach/Tofu Gnocchi:

½ block	firm or extra-firm water-packed tofu that was put in towel with weight on it for a few minutes before crumbling with a fork. Set aside.
6 oz.	spinach leaves, wilted in hot water
½ cup	all-purpose flour
1 tsp.	salt
¼ tsp.	basil
¼ tsp.	garlic powder
¼ tsp.	onion powder

Directions:

1 Squeeze out every drop of water on the spinach with a towel

2 Put spinach on a cookie sheet to dry for 15 minutes. Finely cut the spinach.

3 Mix spinach with crumbled tofu. Set aside.

4 Mix the following in a bowl: flour, salt, basil, garlic powder, and onion powder.

5 Add the crumbled tofu and spinach, stir together, and form into a ball.

6 Divide the dough into 4 equal balls.

7 Shape each ball into an 18-inch rope of dough. Cut the rope into 1-inch pieces.

8 With the back of a fork, press the 1-inch "pillow" of dough up against the fork to leave the characteristic ridges on one side and an indention on the other.

9 Place the small "pillows" in a bowl and lightly dust with flour, to keep the gnocchi separated.

10 Store in a covered container in freezer until ready to boil.

11 Heat water to a slow boil.

12 Drop gnocchi into water; it will rise when done (2 minutes).

13 Ladle to a colander and drain.

14 Cook gnocchi in small batches.

15 Combine gnocchi with garlic cream sauce, pesto sauce, marinara sauce, or a mixture of olive oil, Italian seasoning, and Vegan Parmesan Cheese (p. 125).

NOTE:

You can also bake the spinach/tofu gnocchi in the oven for 12 to 14 minutes on 350° F instead of boiling in water.

Pizza

Makes 4 Servings

prepared Pizza Dough (p. 83)

spaghetti sauce (your favorite)

> chopped olives, black and green
>
> chopped onions
>
> chopped bell pepper
>
> sliced mushrooms
>
> sliced tomatoes
>
> shredded Vegan Gourmet Mozzarella
>
> garlic salt to sprinkle on pizza
>
> vegan parmesan cheese to sprinkle on top of pizza

Directions:

1. I put ingredients on a precooked pizza crust in the above order, leaving the mozzarella for the last topping.

2. Sprinkle a little garlic salt and vegan parmesan cheese on top and put back in the oven at 350°F for 5 minutes.

3. Turn the oven to *broil*. Broil will melt the Vegan Gourmet Mozzarella. You must watch it very closely as it will burn if you are not watching it and get distracted.

4. Set a timer for 4 minutes, or until mozzerella melts and bubbles.

NOTE:

It does melt beautifully if you are a careful cook.

If you do not have Vegan Gourmet Mozzarella, you can use the Garlic Cream Sauce (p. 63) or Deb's Notso Cheeze (p. 47), as they both make nice toppings, but not as realistic as the melted Vegan Gourmet.

INVEST TIME IN OTHERS

Make this recipe a part of your weekend dining experience: invite friends, but don't tell them it's plant-based.

Italian Garlic Cream Sauce

Makes 4 Servings

(To use on various types of pasta)

⅓ cup	Earth Balance natural buttery spread (or margarine)
¼ cup (heaping)	unbleached all-purpose flour
½ cup	Silk soy creamer (if not available, use Silk soymilk (plain)
½ cup	Silk soymilk (plain)
½ cup	Tofutti Better Than Sour Cream
1 tsp.	garlic salt
4	garlic cloves, minced

Directions:

1 Sauté garlic in Earth Balance natural buttery spread.

2 Add flour and stir. Add the rest of the ingredients and keep stirring.

3 This is the basic cream sauce; you may add your favorite optional ingredients now. Then serve on any pasta.

NOTE:

Optional ingredients:
Marinated dried tomato halves, roasted red peppers (find one that contains no vinegar; it tastes much better), pine nuts, sautéed squash, zucchini, mushrooms, fresh spinach leaves, and artichoke hearts are a few suggestions.

Mixing the Garlic Cream Sauce with your favorite marinara sauce is another delicious option.

EDUCATE YOURSELF

In a 2010 Virginia Tech University study of adults aged 55 to 75, drinking two 8-ounce glasses of water before meals was associated with almost 4 pounds more weight loss in 12 weeks than in a control group who ate a similar diet but didn't have the premeal H_2O. Participants drank an average of 1.5 cups of water a day before the study.

Manicotti

Makes 4 Servings

1	large casserole dish (13" x 9") sprayed with Pam
9	manicotti shells (cook according to package directions, drain, set aside to cool).

Directions:

1 pkg.	Mori-nu Silken Tofu firm, mashed
2 tbsp.	Tofutti Sour Cream
¼ tsp.	salt
½ pkg.	frozen spinach, thawed (drain out liquid) or fresh cooked
1	small onion, chopped, cooked in water in the microwave and drained
1 pkg.	Better Than Cream Cheese french onion (or use plain cream cheese and add 1 package of onion soup mix to get the same thing)
1 tube	Ritz crackers, crushed
¼ cup	flaxseed meal

Directions:

1. Mix the above well and stuff the precooked manicotti shells with the filling.

2. Sauce: your favorite spaghetti sauce. Add the following items to spaghetti sauce to give it a better flavor:

3. Sautéed chopped onions and bell peppers, minced garlic, 1 tsp. basil, 1 tsp. oregano (sauté in water for less calories)

4. Place filled manicotti shells in casserole dish and pour sauce evenly over filled shells.

5. Cover with foil and bake 30 minutes at 350°F. Uncover and continue to bake 5 or 10 more minutes.

6. Garnish with sprinkle of fresh chopped basil leaves and Vegan Parmesan Cheese (p. 125).

7. Serve with garlic green beans and a salad.

NOTE:

To make garlic green beans:
Cook Earth Balance buttery spread, 2 to 3 minced garlic cloves, fresh or frozen green beans in a frying pan until done. Sprinkle with garlic salt to taste.

TRUST MORE, STRESS LESS

Stress inhibits proper digestion. Avoid stressful conversations before, during, and after mealtime.

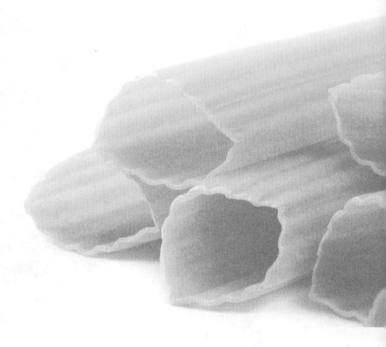

Basil Pesto

Makes 4 Servings

Ingredients:

2 cups	packed fresh basil leaves
¼ cup + 2 tbsp.	pine nuts
2 tbsp.	almond slivers
2 large	garlic cloves
½ tsp.	salt
⅓ cup	olive oil
2 tbsp.	Vegan Parmesan Cheese (add this after you remove the pesto from the food processor)

NOTE:
Use a food processor for best results.

Directions:

1. Chop/pulse the basil, pine nuts, slivered almonds, garlic, and salt.

2. Slowly add the oil into the processor through the feed tube.

3. Remove the pesto from the processor and place in a bowl. Stir in the Vegan Parmesan Cheese (p. 125). This should make about 1 cup of pesto, enough for approximately 1 pound of pasta.

4. Drain most of the liquid from your favorite pasta. (Save part of the liquid in a separate container to help mix if needed, just add by spoonfuls.)

5. Mix in ½ cup for ½ pound of pasta. Or add a small amount at a time until you get the flavor and look you want.

NOTE:
If you have any leftover pesto you can freeze it in empty ice cube trays or in large spoonfuls on wax paper. Remove it later and drop in a small ziplock bag that has been labeled with a permanent marker with the date and "pesto."

You can remove it for later use in: pasta, Eggplant Pesto Parmesan (p. 75), soup, marinara sauce, as grilled sandwich spread, potatoes, toasted French bread. It is best to let the pesto thaw on the countertop, as it becomes hard and crusty quickly in the microwave.

If using a blender instead of a food processor, blend the oil with all the ingredients except the parmesan cheese, which is added after the mixture is taken out of the blender.

Veggies and Spinach Lasagna With Marinara Sauce

Makes 8 Servings

Preheat Oven to 350°F (spray Pam on a 9" x 13" casserole dish)

1 container (16 oz.)	water-packed tofu-firm, drained, and crumbled
2½ cups	Deb's Notso Cheeze (p. 47)
1	onion, chopped
1	bell pepper, chopped
2 cloves	garlic, minced
2	zucchini or 2 yellow squash, chopped (or 1 of each)
3 cups	fresh spinach
1 jar (2 lb. 13 oz.)	your favorite spaghetti sauce
1½ tsp.	basil
1½ tsp.	oregano
	lasagna noodles (dry or hydrated, depending on when you need to serve it)
2	spring onions, chopped, for garnish
½ cup	black olives, sliced, for garnish

Directions:

1 Mix ½ cup Deb's Notso Cheeze with ½ cup spaghetti sauce and set aside to use as the last topping on the lasagna.

2 Sauté onion, bell pepper, garlic, zucchini, and spinach in water until soft.

3 Add spaghetti sauce, basil, and oregano.

4 Add Deb's Notso Cheeze and crumbled tofu. Mix well.

5 Layer marinara, cheese, lasagna starting with vegetable mixture in bottom of baking dish.

6 Layer marinara mixture with lasagna noodles. Repeat steps 5 and 6 again, ending with the mixture

of Deb's Notso Cheeze and spaghetti sauce.

NOTE:

If using uncooked dry noodles, place in refrigerator with the sauce and veggies layered overnight, then bake the next day, which makes the noodles more flavorful as they absorb the seasonings.

To bake and eat immediately, you must follow the directions on the package to soften the noodles by boiling.

7 Cover and bake 350°F for 40 minutes.

8 Garnish with chopped spring onions and black olives.

9 Serve with corn on the cob and salad.

10 Optional: 1 cup sliced mushrooms sautéed in water, added to the veggies and sauce.

EDUCATE YOURSELF

Read a few health resources (such as *The China Study* or *Diet for a New America)* that reveal the benefits of a plant-based diet.

Lasagna With Garlic Cream Sauce

Makes 12 Servings

Preheat Oven to 350°F, spray Pam on 9" x 13" casserole dish. Halve the ingredient portions for 7" x 11" casserole dish.

⅔ cup	Earth Balance natural buttery spread
4 tbsp.	garlic, minced
⅔ cup	unbleached all-purpose flour
3 cups	Silk soymilk (plain)
2 (12.3 oz.)	containers Mori-nu Silken Tofu (soft or firm, either will work)
1 cup	Tofutti Better Than Sour Cream
2 tbsp.	garlic salt
½ tsp.	McKay's Chicken-Style Seasoning or Bill's Best Chick'Nish seasoning
9 to 12 oz.	fresh spinach, just barely steamed and drained
4	medium size yellow squash, sliced and lightly steamed
2	medium- to large-size peeled carrots, chopped into small pieces ½-inch or less sizes, steamed or cooked in microwave until soft
1 box	lasagna noodles

Garnish the top of the lasagna with:

1 tube	Ritz crackers, crushed and combined with
4 tbsp.	Earth Balance buttery spread, melted

Directions:

1 Place ⅔ cup buttery spread in a large skillet; add garlic and sauté. Set aside.

2 Blend the following in the blender: 1½ cups soymilk, ⅔ cup flour, 1 container tofu, 2 tbsp. garlic salt, chicken-style seasoning.

3 Pour this mixture out of the blender and into a large pan, add the sautéed garlic.

4 Next, blend the remaining 1½ cups soymilk, 1 container of tofu, and 1 cup sour cream. Pour this mixture into the frying pan with the sauté garlic.

5 Turn heat to medium or medium-high and stir until thickened.

6 It should be smooth and creamy (if it gets lumpy, return it to the blender). Turn stovetop heat off.

7 Stir in the spinach, squash, and carrots.

Now you are ready to layer this mixture with the lasagna noodles.

8 Boil the lasagna noodles according to the directions if you plan to bake the lasagna within a few hours. If you are going to bake the lasagna the next day, you do not need to boil the noodles as they will absorb the moisture and plump up during the 8 hours it's in the refrigerator.

9 Layer as follows: Put sauce on the bottom of casserole, then noodles, then sauce, ending with sauce on top of the noodles.

10 Sprinkle buttery Ritz crackers on top. This topping gives the perfect accent to a creamy dish!

11 Bake uncovered at 350°F for 40 minutes.

12 Serve with green beans and salad.

NOTE:
This does not freeze well.

Macaroni and Cheese

Makes 4 Servings

Preheat Oven to 350°F

2 cups	macaroni noodles (preferably whole-wheat)
1½ cups	Deb's Notso Cheeze (p. 47)
⅓ cup	onion, finely chopped
1½ cups	Silk soymilk (plain)
½ tsp.	salt
½ tsp.	onion salt
½ tsp.	basil
1 to 2 tbsp.	Earth Balance buttery spread

EXERCISE

Walking is one of the best ways to burn fat, as it requires constant oxygen, which in turn burns fat. Try walking after each meal.

Directions:

1 Cook macaroni according to directions. Drain.

2 In medium bowl mix macaroni, Notso Cheeze, onion, soymilk, and seasonings.

3 The milk should come to just about the level of the macaroni in the dish. (You may need to add more soymilk; it just depends on the level of the milk in the dish.)

4 1-2 tbsp. Earth Balance buttery spread smoothed onto the top layer of the macaroni and cheese.

5 Bake 350°F for 30 minutes, covered.

6 Serve with vegetarian baked beans and broccoli.

Eggplant Pesto Parmesan

Makes 6 Servings
Preheat Oven to 375° F, spray 9" x 13" casserole dish with Pam

Eggplant:

1	large eggplant, peeled and sliced into ¼-inch-thick slices
1+ cup	Silk soymilk (plain)
1+ cup	Panko Japanese Bread Flakes (or crumbs)
2 tbsp.	nutritional yeast flakes

Filling:

Basil Pesto (p. 67)

1+ cup	Tofutti Soy Sour Cream

Marinara Sauce

Makes 6 Servings

1 jar (24 oz.)	your favorite spaghetti sauce
	water for sautéeing
1	onion, chopped
2	garlic cloves, minced
½ tsp.	oregano
½ tsp.	basil
2	bay leaves

Directions:

1 Place eggplant slices in soymilk to soak.

2 In a separate bowl, mix Panko Bread Flakes and nutritional yeast flakes.

3 Put wire rack on baking sheet to allow even baking of the eggplant once it is breaded.

4 Take eggplant slices and dredge in Panko mixture.

5 Press bread crumbs on eggplant.

6 Place eggplant slices on wire rack and bake at 375°F for 35 minutes.

7 Remove from oven and set aside. They should be crispy.

8 After baking eggplant, turn oven temperature down to 350°F.

9 Sauté onion and garlic in water until soft. (Put enough water to cover the bottom of the pan to prevent burning of onion.)

10 Add marinara sauce and the rest of the seasonings (oregano, basil, and bay leaves). Bring to a boil, then turn off heat.

11 Remove bay leaves from marinara sauce. Spoon a small amount of marinara sauce in bottom of casserole dish, just to barely cover the bottom of the dish.

12 Layer eggplant slices over pasta sauce, and place a small amount of basil pesto on each eggplant.

13 Place a spoonful of sour cream on top of the basil pesto.

14 Smooth out mixture so it covers the entire top of the breaded eggplant.

15 Layer a small amount of sauce on top of the sour cream.

16 Layer remaining eggplant slices, following the same procedure: basil pesto, sour cream, ending with marinara sauce.

17 Bake at 350°F for 40 to 50 minutes.

18 Garnish with Vegan Parmesan Cheese (p.125).

19 Serve with asparagus or broccoli, salad, and garlic bread.

WATER

"Your internal thermostat works better when you're well hydrated," Duke nutritionist Beth Reardon says. "Water helps regulate body temperature." Drink up.

Cindy's Caprese Panino

Makes 2 Servings

extra virgin olive oil

large bakery loaf of flat bread (french, ciabatta, focaccia, etc.)

Vegan Gourmet Mozzarella, sliced ⅛-inch thick

tomatoes, sliced ¼-inch thick

Basil Pesto (p. 67)

fresh mushrooms, sliced

green olives, sliced

black olives, sliced

fresh basil leaves

roasted red peppers, fresh or in a jar

salt to taste

Directions:

1 Cut bread in half lengthwise.

2 Lightly brush both sides of bread with olive oil.

3 Place the half of bread cut side up on a grill or skillet.

4 Layer vegetables and salt on bread in above order.

5 Top with the other half of the sliced flat bread.

6 If using an electric grill, set temperature on 300°F.

7 If you do not have a grill, heat on medium temperature in a fry pan to melt cheese and heat up veggies.

8 Place a heavy pan on top of the flat bread and press down. (This will look like a *thick* sandwich.)

9 Cook for 3 to 4 minutes. Remove heavy pan.

10 Turn sandwich over very carefully.

11 Place a heavy pan on top of the flat bread and press down again.

12 Cook for 3 minutes. The bread will become toasty, crusty, and less thick.

13 Remove pan on top of flat bread. Turn off heating element.

14 Carefully slide onto a serving plate and slice in half.

15 Serve immediately while cheese is melted and sandwich is hot.

NOTE:
One of the keys to this delicious sandwich is the Basil Pesto and fresh basil leaves; the aroma is fantastic as the veggies heat up. It makes the sandwich oh, so good.

Veggie Burgers

Makes 12 Patties
Preheat Oven to 350°F

1 can (19 oz.)	Loma Linda Vege-Burger
1 can (15 oz.)	garbanzos, processed in food processor
½ cup	walnuts, chopped
½ cup	rolled oats
3 tbsp.	flaxseed meal
2 tbsp.	gluten flour
½ tube	Ritz cracker crumbs (more or less)
⅓ cup	Deb's Notso Cheeze (p. 47)
1	onion, finely chopped
1	bell pepper, finely chopped
2 tbsp.	Bragg's Liquid Aminos
1 tbsp.	whole-wheat flour
1 tsp.	Bill's Best Chick'Nish
½ tsp.	garlic salt
¼ tsp.	garlic powder

Directions:

1 Combine all above ingredients and form into patties.

2 Bake 25 minutes. Serve in a sandwich with lettuce, tomato, onion, avocado, and Vegenaise.

NOTE:
You can substitute ⅓ cup Tofutti Sour Cream in place of Deb's Cheeze.

Use a wide mouth canning jar ring to make 12 perfect-sized burgers.

Veggie Burgers freeze well.

Vegenaise is a mayonnaise substitute purchased at whole foods stores.

WATER

Water is filling, so you feel fuller and eat less. Those who drink water 30 minutes to 1 hour before meals consume an average of 75 fewer calories per meal.

Bean Burgers

Makes 6-7 Patties
Preheat Oven to 350°F

1 can (16 oz.)	beans, drained and mashed (pinto, black, fat-free refried beans, garbanzo, or white beans)
½ cup	walnuts, chopped
½ cup	onion, finely chopped
½ cup	bell pepper, finely chopped
2 tbsp.	flaxseed meal
2 tbsp.	whole-wheat flour
1 tbsp.	Bragg's Liquid Aminos
1 tsp.	Bill's Best Chick'Nish seasoning
¼ tsp.	cumin
½ tsp.	onion powder
½ tsp.	garlic powder
½ tsp.	garlic salt
½ tube	Ritz crackers

NOTE:
Half to a whole tube Ritz Crackers, adjust as needed to form patties.

Directions:

1 Combine all the above ingredients and form into patties.

2 Bake 25 minutes. Makes 7 patties. Serve in a sandwich with lettuce, tomato, onion, avocado, and Vegenaise. Freeze leftover patties if you will not be using them in 2 days.

NOTE:
If using refried beans, add more Ritz Crackers.

Use a wide mouth canning jar ring to make perfect burgers.

Bean Burgers freeze well.

See "Almonaise" for vegan mayonnaise substitute. (p. 125)

If patty mixture needs more moisture to form into patties, add up to ⅓ cup Deb's Notso Cheeze or Sour Cream to the ingredients.

Croutons

Makes 4 Servings

4 slices	bread cut into ½-inch cubes
	extra virgin olive oil
¾-1 tsp.	garlic salt or to your taste
1 tsp.	Italian seasoning

Directions:

1 Place bread cubes on cookie sheet and spray with olive oil.

2 Sprinkle seasonings on bread. Bake at 325°F for 8 minutes; stir and cook another 5 minutes or until dry and crunchy.

NOTE:
If wanting a lower salt crouton, try using garlic powder, onion powder, or nutritional yeast flakes as an alternative.

You can drizzle olive oil on the croutons and toss if olive oil spray is not available. I put olive oil in a pump spray can that you can purchase in stores that sell kitchen accessories.

NUTRITION

Digestion requires 4½ to 5 hours digestion time. For good health, avoid snacking and eating in between meals.

Pizza Dough

Makes 1 Pizza

NOTE:

If you are not using real cheese, it is very important to make your own dough to give it a wonderful appealing taste.

1 cup	Silk soymilk
1 cup	oats
2 tbsp.	honey (or another sugar)
1 tbsp. or 1 pkg.	Rapid Rise Highly Active Yeast
¼ cup	olive oil, plus extra for shaping dough
1 tsp.	salt
1 heaping tbsp.	dried Italian seasoning
1 cup	whole-wheat flour
1 cup	unbleached all-purpose flour
1 tbsp.	vital wheat gluten

Directions:

1 Heat soymilk in the microwave until hot. Add oats and honey.

2 When the soymilk cools down and is warm, add yeast and stir well.

3 You want the yeast to begin to foam a little; this takes a few minutes.

4 Add oil, salt, and Italian seasoning.

5 Mix together.

6 Slowly add the wheat, white flour, and wheat gluten, mixing together until it becomes a soft dough.

7 Knead for 5 to 10 minutes.

8 Spray a 14-inch pizza pan with vegetable spray and put dough on the pan. Drizzle several drops of olive oil on top of the dough and smooth over the surface of the dough.

9 Roll the pizza dough out to the edges of the pizza pan with a rolling pin. Lightly spray with olive oil or Pam, then place wax paper on top of the dough. This will keep the dough from drying out while it is rising. Next, take a kitchen towel and wet it in water, wring it out, and place on the wax paper that is on the pizza dough. The towel adds just the right moisture to aid in rising.

10 Place pizza pan with dough in a warm oven.

11 Let the dough rise until double in size in the oven (this may take 1 hour +).

12 After dough has risen, remove the towel and wax paper. Increase the oven temp to 350°F and bake for 15 to 20 minutes or until lightly golden.

13 Remove from oven. Baking the dough before putting the pizza ingredients on gives you a better crust and less chance for it to become "soggy."

NOTE:

See the Pizza recipe (p. 61) to add sauce and toppings.

Apple Muffins

Makes 12 Muffins

Preheat Oven to 350°F

Topping:

3 tbsp.	melted or softened Earth Balance buttery spread
3 tbsp.	florida crystals
⅓ cup	pecans, chopped
⅓ cup	whole-wheat flour
¼ cup	white all-purpose flour
2 tbsp.	wheat germ, toasted

Mix topping ingredients together and set aside.

2 cups	peeled chopped apples (gala or sweet apples work best)
1 cup	whole-wheat flour
¼ cup	all-purpose flour
1 cup	florida crystals
½ cup	chopped pecans
¼ cup	flaxseed meal
1 tbsp.	Ener-G baking powder
½ tsp.	salt
½ tsp.	ground cinnamon (or ground coriander)
½ cup	applesauce

Directions for Muffins:

1 Mix the dry ingredients together.

2 Stir in apples and applesauce.

3 The mixture will be dry with chunks of apple, but the apple chunks will form more liquid as it bakes to give the extra moisture it needs.

4 Spoon mixture into 12 pre-sprayed muffin forms.

Directions for Topping:

1 Spoon topping on each muffin before baking.

2 Sprinkle the topping onto each muffin. Do not press, as it will become hard and brittle during the baking process. The light sprinkling gives a very appetizing appearance!

3 Bake 350°F for 35 minutes or until toothpick comes out clean.

4 Very tasty warm. Try warming up in the microwave before serving if you do not eat them right away.

EDUCATE YOURSELF

Vegetarian diets have been shown to reduce one's chances of forming kidney stones and gallstones. Diets that are high in protein, especially animal protein, tend to cause the body to excrete more calcium, oxalate, and uric acid. These three substances are the main components of urinary tract stones. British researchers have advised that persons with a tendancy to form kidney stones should follow a vegetarian diet.

Bran Muffins

Makes 12 Muffins

Preheat Oven to 350°F

1 cup	100 percent apple juice
¼ cup	maple syrup
20	dates, pitted (1¼ cups). Cut each date in half to ensure pits are gone.
½ cup	applesauce (unsweetened)
2 tbsp.	molasses
¼ cup	flaxseed meal
1 cup	whole-wheat flour
½ cup	all-purpose unbleached flour
½ cup	walnuts, chopped
⅓ cup	wheat bran
⅓ cup	oat bran
½ tsp.	salt
2½ tsp.	Ener-G baking powder

Topping (optional):

3 tbsp.	melted or softened Earth Balance buttery spread
3 tbsp.	florida crystals
⅓ cup	pecans, chopped
⅓ cup	whole-wheat flour
3 tbsp.	wheat germ, toasted

Mix the topping ingredients together and set aside.

Directions:

1. Mix apple juice, maple syrup, dates, applesauce, and molasses in blender. Set aside.
2. Put remaining ingredients in a bowl and stir to mix together.
3. Pour wet ingredients into dry ingredients.
4. Spoon into 12 muffin containers.
5. Sprinkle 1 tablespoon topping on each muffin.
6. *Do not* press topping down on mixture. Pressing it down makes it hard, and it has a better appearance "crumbly."
7. Bake 25 minutes or until toothpick comes out clean.

NOTE:

You can also add ½ cup raisins.

> **NUTRITION**
>
> Morning breakfast is the time to break your "fast." Don't skip breakfast. Having a large breakfast actually helps you lose weight.

Corn Bread Muffins

Makes 12 Muffins

1⅓ cups	plain cornmeal
½ cup	all-purpose flour
2 tbsp.	cornstarch
1 tbsp.	flaxseed meal
½ tsp.	salt
1 can (14 oz.)	creamed corn
2 tbsp.	soymilk powder (any brand of tofu or soymilk powder)
¼ cup	Silk soymilk (plain)
¼ cup	maple syrup
1 tbsp.	lemon juice concentrate
2½ tbsp.	Ener-G baking powder

Directions:

1 Mix together cornmeal, flour, cornstarch, flaxseed meal, and salt. Set aside.

2 Whisk together creamed corn, soymilk, soymilk powder, and maple syrup.

3 Add lemon juice and stir well (this makes a Mock Buttermilk).

4 Combine cornmeal flour mixture and creamed corn mixture, stir.

5 Stir in baking powder last.

6 Spoon into muffin containers sprayed with Pam.

7 Bake in 375°F oven 25 minutes or until toothpick comes out of muffin clean.

NOTE:

Try this with the recipe Sweet Bread Spread (p.121).

You can add 2 to 3 tablespoons chopped green chiles and ¼ teaspoon ground red pepper to give a *mild* degree of spice. Adding more of these ingredients will kick up the "heat."

Whole kernel corn in water will *not* work as a substitute for creamed corn.

EDUCATE YOURSELF

Harvard studies that included tens of thousands of women and men have shown that regular meat consumption increases colon cancer risk by roughly 300 percent.

Danish Pecan Rolls

Makes 12 Servings

1½ cups	hot Silk soymilk (plain)
1 cup	old-fashioned rolled oats
1 tsp.	salt
¼ cup	vegetable oil
2 tbsp.	maple syrup
2 tbsp.	yeast
1½ cups	unbleached all-purpose white flour, (and for sprinkling work surface)
1 cup	whole-wheat flour
¼ cup	Earth Balance buttery spread
2 tbsp.	agave (can substitute honey)
¼ cup + 2 tbsp.	florida crystals
1+ tsp.	cinnamon or coriander
1 cup	pecans, chopped
½ cup	raisins (optional)

Directions:

1 Combine hot soymilk, oats, salt, oil, 2 tablespoons maple syrup. Stir well.

2 When soymilk cools to warm temperature, add yeast. Set aside.

3 When this mixture starts to foam and bubble, add white flour and wheat flour.

4 Stir and make a soft dough. (You do not need to knead this dough.)

5 Put dough onto a floured surface. Roll out to approximate 10" x 13" rectangle.

6 Smooth buttery spread over the surface of the dough rectangle.

7 Smooth 2 tablespoons agave nectar over the buttery spread-covered dough. (This works better than maple syrup because it is not as runny and sticks to the dough surface better.)

8 Spread florida crystals over the dough.

9 Sprinkle cinnamon (or coriander), pecans, and/or raisins next.

10 Roll dough up longwise.

11 Cut into 1 to 1½-inch sections with a long sewing thread by putting the thread under the end and bringing up each end of the thread and crossing the top. This will make approximately 16 one-inch rolls.

12 Place rolls in a 9" x 13" casserole dish sprayed with Pam.

13 Let rise in a warm oven (125°F) for 20 to 30 minutes.

14 Turn the oven temperature up to 350°F and set the timer for 20 to 30 minutes.

15 While the cinnamon rolls are baking, combine the ingredients for the icing.

Icing

2 tbsp.	cornstarch
2 tbsp.	Earth Balance buttery spread
2 tbsp.	agave (can substitute maple syrup)
1 tbsp.	all-purpose unbleached flour
1 tbsp.	Silk soymilk (plain)
½ cup	florida crystals
⅛ tsp.	vanilla extract

Directions:

1 Combine above ingredients in a pan. Turn heat to medium until thickened.

2 Remove Danish Pecan Rolls from the oven and pour icing on top of rolls. Sprinkle 1 cup chopped pecans on top of the icing.

Split Pea Soup

Makes 6 Servings

2 cups	dry green split peas
2 quarts	water
½	medium fresh onion, chopped
1 cup	cooked whole barley or brown rice
1 tbsp.	salt
1 tsp.	basil
	garlic salt to taste

WATER

The amount of water to drink has a formula: Divide your weight by two and drink half your body weight in ounces.

Directions:

1 Wash and sort peas, add water, bring to boil and turn off heat.

2 Cover pan with lid and let stand 1 hour.

3 Drain water off and rinse peas.

4 Cover peas with water by 1 to 2 inches.

5 Bring heat back up to medium high; add onion and then cover the pot.

6 When the peas begin to boil, stir and turn temp down to medium and return lid. Cook covered for 2½ to 3 hours or until peas are soft and easily crushed. Put peas in blender and process until smooth (may need to add more water to blend).

7 Return to pan and add cooked barley or brown rice, basil, and salt.

8 Add garlic salt to taste.

9 Add additional water for thick or thinness of soup, and garnish with Croutons (p. 81).

Amazon Lentil Soup

Makes 6 Servings

2 cups	dry lentils
6 to 8 cups	water
1 tbsp.	salt
½ tsp.	garlic salt
⅛ tsp.	ground red pepper
1	medium fresh onion, chopped
2	large garlic cloves, minced
2	bay leaves
2	large white potatoes, chopped and cooked
½ bunch	fresh cilantro, chopped
1	carrot, chopped, cooked
2 cups	your favorite spaghetti sauce
1 cup	textured vegetable protein (tvp) unflavored chuck (marinated in ½ cup all natural Bragg's Liquid Aminos or soy sauce for at least 30 minutes)

Directions:

1 Wash and sort lentils, add water, bring to boil and turn off heat.

2 Cover pan with lid and let stand 1 hour. Drain water off and rinse lentils. Add fresh water to cover lentils by 1 to 2 inches.

3 Bring heat back up to medium high; add bay leaves, garlic, onion, cilantro, potatoes, carrot, marinated tvp, and lid to the pot.

4 When the lentils begin to boil, stir and turn temperature down to medium heat and return lid. Cook covered until done with desired tenderness (about 20+ minutes).

5 Add spaghetti sauce, salt, red pepper powder, and simmer until time to serve.

6 Remove bay leaves and serve with crusty bread and a salad.

NUTRITION

Prior to eating this dish, have more fresh, leafy vegetables.

Cream of Potato Soup

Makes 4 Servings

6	large red potatoes (cubed) that have been scrubbed and any blemishes or eyes removed.
1 cup	Silk soymilk (plain)
¼ cup	unbleached all-purpose flour
1 tbsp.	garlic salt
½ cup	Tofutti Soy Sour Cream
3	scallions, chopped (the whole scallion)

NUTRITION

This dish has no cholesterol. Share this delicious taste with someone who has high LDL cholesterol.

Directions:

1 Place potatoes in a large pan.

2 Add water 1 to 2 inches above the potatoes.

3 Bring to boil until tender.

4 Remove from heat.

5 Take ½ of the water out of the pan and save.

6 Blend milk, flour, and half of the potatoes until smooth.

7 Add this to the pot of cooked cubed potatoes.

8 Stir and turn heat to medium.

9 Add Tofutti Soy Sour Cream and continue to stir.

10 Add garlic salt.

11 Add additional "saved water" for desired consistency. Garnish with scallions and serve with a salad.

Creamy Butternut Squash Soup

Makes 4 Servings

4 cups	butternut squash, cooked
2	potatoes microwaved, discard skins, and cut into chunks
½ cup	cashews (dry roasted)
4½ cups	water, divided (see directions)

Directions:

1 Blend ½ cup cashews with 1½ cups water until smooth. Add 1 cup squash and blend again.

2 Add half the potato chunks and continue blending. (You may add water as necessary to blend.)

3 You may need to pour part of the blended squash into a pot.

4 Continue blending the rest of the squash, potatoes, and water until the above ingredients are blended.

5 Pour blended mixture into a pot.

Add below listed seasonings into the pot and turn heat to medium-high.

1 tsp.	salt (may add more, adjust to your taste)
½ tsp.	basil
½ tsp.	Bill's Best Chik'Nish seasoning

Cook until just beginning to boil, and then add:

1 cup	Cooked Potato Gnocchi (p. 57).
	Serve with Croutons (p. 81).

NOTE:
Potato gnocchi is available to purchase in grocery stores and whole food stores if you do not have time to make it yourself.

Follow cooking instructions, add cooked gnocchi to the soup, heat, and eat.

"This is day 21, and I've lost 25 pounds. Wow, this has been a great experience. Friends and coworkers see many positive changes and are asking questions."
— Pamela

Hearty Black Bean Soup

Makes 4 Servings

2 cans (15 oz.)	black beans
2 cups	cooked rice
½	chopped onion, reserve 2+ tbsp. for garnish
½	bell pepper, chopped
3-4	garlic cloves, minced
1	scallion, chopped
¼ cup	cilantro, chopped
1 tsp.	garlic salt
½ tsp.	garlic powder
¼ tsp.	ground red pepper
½ tsp.	cumin
1 can (14.5 oz.)	diced tomatoes that have been blended in a blender
1 cup	water (divide into ¼ and ¾ cups)
1 tbsp.	all-purpose flour
½	avocado, diced for garnish
¼ cup	Tofutti Sour Cream for garnish
½	tomato, chopped for garnish

I took The New Life Challenge with my mother, who was having some serious health issues. It was the beginning of a healthier life. I not only had a weight loss of 24 pounds, but found myself thinking much clearer and having more energy. We saw some wonderful results in my mother's health. The principles laid out in this book have changed our lives forever.
—Johanna Farrar

Directions:

1   Sauté onions, bell pepper, and garlic in ¼ cup water in a skillet on medium-high heat. When cooked, add chopped scallion and seasonings. Stir and set aside.

2   Combine blended tomatoes, 2 cans of beans with liquid, and the sautéed veggies into a pot on the stove. Stir and heat until steaming.

3   Take 1 cup bean soup, ¾ cup water, and 1 tablespoon flour and process in blender until smooth, then return to the pot of bean soup.

4   Stir and heat until boiling.

To serve:

5   Place ¼ to ½ cup rice in bowl, then add black bean soup. Top with sour cream, diced avocado, chopped tomato, and chopped onion. Serve with a salad.

Vegetable Garden Stew

Makes 6 Servings

1	onion, chopped
2 cloves	garlic, minced
1	stalk celery, chopped
2	carrots, chopped
2	potatoes, cubed
2 cups	cabbage, shredded
½ cup	green beans, frozen or canned
½ cup	corn, frozen or canned
2	bay leaves
3+ cups	water, divided into 1½ cups
1 cup+	your favorite spaghetti sauce
1 can	northern beans, rinsed and drained
1½ tsp.	garlic salt
½ tsp.	onion powder
½ tsp.	garlic powder
1 tsp.	McKay's Beef-Style Seasoning
1 tsp.	basil
2 tbsp.	Bragg's Liquid Aminos
1 tbsp.	ketchup
⅛ tsp.	ground red pepper

Directions:

1 Place onion, garlic, celery, carrots, potatoes, cabbage, green beans, corn, bay leaves, and 1½ cups water in stockpot on medium-high heat.

2 Cook until tender with the lid on the stockpot.

3 Add water, spaghetti sauce, northern beans, and seasonings.

4 Cook on medium heat about 10 minutes.

NOTE:

(This is a good time to add any leftovers in your refrigerator, for example: squash, beans, rice, or pasta).

You may add more water for your desired consistency. (I like a thick consistency.)

Serve corn bread muffins with Sweet Bread Spread (p. 121).

Frozen or fresh cut okra should always be added near the end of cooking so it doesn't get soft and tacky.

NUTRITION

Blood is needed for digesting food, drawing from the brain. These meals will require much help. Stay sharp by eating less.

Maple-Banzo Waffles

Makes 3 Servings

1 cup	soaked garbanzos (½ cup dried)
1½ cups	Silk soymilk
½ cup +1 tbsp.	whole-wheat flour
½ cup	unbleached all-purpose flour
2 tbsp.	flaxseed meal
3 tbsp.	maple syrup
1 tsp.	vanilla extract
½ tsp.	salt

Directions:

1 Blend above ingredients together.

2 Bake in hot waffle iron (sprayed with Pam).

3 Make sure you spray Pam on the waffle iron before pouring each waffle.

NOTE:

Freezes well. Toasts well.

If using canned garbanzos, alter the recipe as follows:
Use ¾ cup canned garbanzos and add 2 tablespoons of whole-wheat flour instead of just adding 1 tablespoon of whole-wheat flour.

Serve with Earth Balance buttery spread, peanut butter, Fruit Sauce Toppings (p. 113), fresh fruit, and/or maple syrup.

INVEST TIME IN OTHERS

Helping others is associated with higher levels of mental health, above and beyond the benefits of receiving help, and other known psycho-spiritual, stress, and demographic factors.

Pancakes

Makes 5 Servings

1½ cups	all-purpose unbleached flour
1 cup	whole-wheat flour
¼ cup	flaxseed meal
1 tbsp.	wheat germ
3 tbsp.	Ener-G baking powder
1 tsp.	salt
2 cups	soymilk (may need to add ¼ cup more, as it thickens when sitting)
¼ cup	maple syrup + 2 tbsp. maple syrup
2 tsp.	vanilla

Directions:

1. Mix dry ingredients and set aside.
2. Mix wet ingredients. Combine wet and dry ingredients.
3. Pour onto hot griddle and flip pancake after bubbles appear in the center of each pancake.
4. Makes 15 pancakes.
5. Serve with maple syrup, chopped pecans, fresh fruit, or see recipe for Fruit Sauce Toppings (p. 113).

Sprouted Wheat Pancakes

Makes 5 Servings

Use the pancake recipe with the following changes:

1 cup — sprouted wheat berries blended in blender with 2 cups soymilk until smooth. Add maple syrup and vanilla, then blend again. Mix together the dry ingredients.

Immediately pour the wet ingredients into the mixed dry ingredients.

Directions:

1 Mix well. Pour pancakes on a griddle or nonstick fry pan sprayed with Pam. (May need to add additional soymilk, as pancake mixture will thicken after pouring the first few pancakes.)

2 Serve with fresh fruit, chopped nuts, Fruit Sauce Toppings (p. 113), or maple syrup.

NUTRITION

Digestion begins in the mouth. Not in the stomach. Chew your food slowly and thoroughly.

Fruit Sauce Toppings

Makes 4 Servings
Use on waffles, pancakes, cheesecake, or ice cream.

Apple Fruit Topping:
2 cups	chopped apples (cored and peeled)
8-10 oz.	unsweetened apple juice

Directions:

1. Mix together. Heat on medium-high heat until steaming, then turn heat to medium for 10 to 15 minutes until apples are cooked. Serve.

2. If you are using tart apples, you may want to use ¼ cup agave nectar or florida crystals.

Apple Berry Fruit Topping:
1 cup	chopped apples (cored and peeled)
1 cup	fresh or frozen raspberries or sliced strawberries
8-10 oz.	apple juice mixed with 1 tbsp. cornstarch
¼ cup	agave nectar or florida crystals.

Directions:

1. Mix apple juice, cornstarch, and agave nectar. Add apples.

2. Heat on medium-high heat until steaming, then turn heat down to medium.

3. Cook until apples are the consistency you like. (My family prefers the apples not completely cooked.)

4. Add berries just before serving so they will keep their shape and texture.

Blueberry Fruit Topping:
2 cups	fresh or frozen blueberries
1 cup	unsweetened apple juice mixed with 2 tbsp. cornstarch
2+ tbsp.	agave nectar (adjust to your taste) (if you do not have agave nectar, substitute ¼ cup florida crystals)

Directions:

Mix together. Heat on medium high heat until steaming. Turn off heat. Serve.

Strawberry or Raspberry Fruit Topping:
2 cups	fresh or frozen strawberries or raspberries
1 cup	apple juice mixed with 2 tbsp. cornstarch
2+ tbsp.	agave nectar (adjust to taste) or florida crystals

Directions:

Mix all the ingredients together and heat on medium-high heat. Stir until it thickens. Serve.

Scrambled Tofu

Makes 3-4 Servings

½ cup	water
½	onion, chopped
½	bell pepper, chopped
½ cup	chopped mushrooms (optional)
1	scallion, chopped

Directions:

1 Sauté the above in water until tender (may need to add more water if mixture gets dry).

2 Add: 1 water-packed container Tofu, drained and crumbled

3 Add:

1 tbsp.	Bill's Best Chik'Nish seasoning
½ tsp.	salt
⅛ tsp.	garlic salt
½	chopped tomato to garnish

4 Heat on medium-high until steaming hot. Garnish with tomatoes. Serve with grits, English potatoes, toast, or biscuits.

NOTE:

When cooking grits, use plain soymilk instead of water in preparation, as it is more creamy and nutritious.

NUTRITION

Prepare this meal, pack it up and enjoy outdoors in the fresh air. Fresh air increases circulation, helping with good digestion.

English Potatoes

Makes 1 serving per potato
Preheat Oven to 375°-400°F

Directions:

1 Use 1 raw large potato with skin on per person.

2 Cut into one-inch cubes.

3 Spray casserole dish with Pam. Add potatoes and several spoonfuls of Earth Balance buttery spread randomly placed into dish.

4 Bake 10 minutes, then stir mixture.

5 Bake additional 10 minutes or so until tender.

6 Remove from oven. Sprinkle with garlic salt to taste.

7 Garnish with chopped scallions.

Creamy Gravy

Makes 4 Servings

2 tbsp.	all-purpose white flour
1¼	Silk soymilk (plain)
¾ tsp.	Bill's Best Chick'Nish seasoning
¾ tsp.	onion powder
¼ tsp.	basil
¼ tsp.	salt

Directions:

1 Combine all ingredients.

2 Cook on medium high until thickened (5 minutes), with constant stirring.

Breakfast Burrito

Makes 4 Servings

6	8-inch flour tortillas or 4 10-inch
	Creamy Gravy (p. 117)
	Scrambled Tofu (p. 115)
6 to 7	baked tater tots per burrito
1 to 2	tomatoes, chopped

Directions:

1 Bake tater tots according to package directions. Set aside.

2 Warm individual tortillas in microwave 6 to 7 seconds.

3 Spoon Creamy Gravy on tortilla and smooth to the edges.

4 Spoon Scrambled Tofu down the center of the tortilla.

5 Cut tater tots in half, place randomly down the center of the tortilla.

6 Scatter chopped tomatoes down the center of the tortilla.

7 Spoon Creamy Gravy down the center of the tortilla.

8 Fold and eat.

NOTE:
Serve with fresh fruit.

ENJOY THE SUNSHINE

Vitamin D doesn't actually come from the sun. The sun converts your good HDL cholesterol into vitamin D. Enjoy these dishes that have no bad cholesterol.

Breakfast Casserole

Makes 6-8 Servings

Preheat Oven to 375°F (spray 9" x 13" casserole dish with Pam)

1	onion, chopped
1	bell pepper, chopped
2 cups	chopped mushrooms (optional)
20	tater tots (about 2 cups)
1	container water-packed firm tofu, drained (wrap tofu in a towel to soak up excess water for a few minutes, then crumble)
1 (12 oz.)	container Tofutti Sour Cream
¼ cup	all-purpose flour
½ tsp.	garlic salt
½ tsp.	salt
⅛ tsp.	turmeric
1½ tsp.	Bill's Best Chick'Nish seasoning
¼ cup	nutritional yeast flakes
1	chopped scallion for garnish
2	small chopped tomatoes, divided (half in the casserole, half set aside as a garnish)

Directions:

1 Bake tater tots according to directions.

2 Cut in half. Set aside.

3 Sauté chopped onion, bell pepper, and mushrooms in water.

4 Mix tofu with sour cream, tomatoes, onions, bell pepper, mushrooms, seasoning, flour, and tater tots.

5 Pour into sprayed casserole dish.

6 Bake 45 minutes.

7 Remove from oven, garnish with scallions and tomatoes.

8 Serve with bran muffins or toast and fresh fruit.

NOTE:

A great way to use your leftover Scrambled Tofu (p. 115)! Just add the leftover tofu when you mix all the ingredients together.

You can make this the day before, put it in the refrigerator, and bake it for breakfast the next morning.

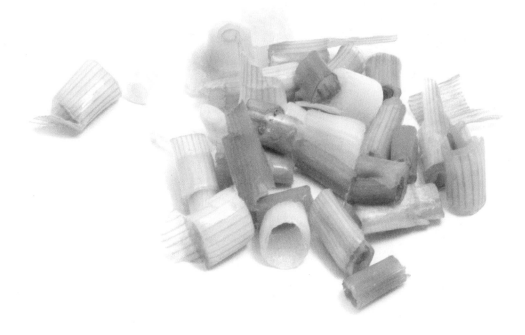

Hot Multigrain Goodness Cereal

Makes 2-3 Servings

3 cups	water
1 cup	rolled oats
¼ cup	steel-cut oats
¼ cup	sprouted whole-wheat (⅛ cup whole-wheat soaked in water overnight, then drained)
¼ cup	sprouted barley (⅛ cup barley soaked in water overnight, then drained)
½ cup	walnuts, chopped
2 tbsp.	soymilk powder
1 tbsp.	flaxseed meal
⅛ tsp.	salt

Directions:

1 Combine rolled oats, steel-cut oats, and water.

2 Cook in pan on medium-high heat 5 minutes with lid on, stirring occasionally. Turn down heat to medium.

3 Stir in the remaining ingredients.

4 Cook 5 more minutes on medium heat.

5 Simmer until ready to eat.

NOTE:

Options:
This cereal is good plain, but you can add your favorite fresh fruit on top before serving.

Here are a few suggestions:
blueberries, strawberries, raspberries, chopped apples (dried fruit, [raisins, dates, apricots, etc.] would also be tasty)

Maple syrup to taste

To get sprouted wheat or barley: soak overnight in container on countertop; drain off liquid the next day. Rinse with water each day. Once it sprouts, put in refrigerator in a covered container. Eat before the sprouts get more than 1/8-inch long, as it gets a more salad taste at that point and not a hot cereal taste. Add maple syrup as needed for a sweeter taste.

Sweet Bread Spread

Makes 4 Servings

¼ cup	Earth Balance buttery spread, softened
1 tbsp.	maple syrup or honey

Directions:

Mix well and serve.

NUTRITION

Enjoy fast food: put oatmeal in a Crockpot at night on low and enjoy the fastest fast food ever the next morning.

Smoothie

Makes 2 Servings

2 cups	orange juice
2	frozen bananas, chopped
1 cup	frozen mango (also try frozen strawberries or blueberries)

Directions:

1. Blend the above until smooth.
2. You can also use apple juice, grape juice, or soymilk instead of orange juice.

NUTRITION

Here is a great evening challenge: drink just a fruit or green smoothie as a final meal in the evening.

Nondairy Sour Cream

Makes 1+ Cups
(a vegan substitute)

1 cup	raw cashews
¼ tsp.	salt (or to your taste)
⅛ tsp.	garlic powder
¼ cup	fresh lemon juice
1¼ cups	boiling water

Directions:

1. Whiz cashews in dry blender.
2. Add boiling water, garlic, and salt, blending continuously.
3. Add fresh lemon juice and whiz on high until smooth and creamy.
4. Chill in refrigerator.

NOTE:

You can substitute Nondairy Sour Cream in the place of Tofutti Sour Cream.

Vegan Parmesan Cheese

Makes 2+ Cups

1 cup	hulled sesame seeds, lightly toasted in oven (or buy hulled *toasted* sesame seeds)

Directions:

Put toasted sesame seeds in blender (blender should be "dry" inside) and add following:

⅔ cup	almond slivers
½ cup	cashews
⅓ cup	yeast flakes

1 tsp.	salt
2 tsp.	onion powder
¼ tsp.	garlic powder

Coarsely mill in blender and store in refrigerator.

Deb's Almonaise

Makes 2+ Cups
(mayonnaise substitute)

2 cups	cold water
1½ cups	blanched almonds (to blanch: place almonds in boiling water for 1 minute, rinse with cold water, squeeze almonds out of skin)
1 clove	fresh garlic
1½ tsp.	salt

Put all the above ingredients in the blender and process until completely smooth.

1 cup	cold-pressed virgin olive oil
½ cup	fresh lemon juice (concentrated lemon juice will not work)

Directions:

1. Continue blending and slowly add olive oil.
2. Next, slowly add fresh lemon juice.
3. Mixture should thicken and lighten in color.
4. Lemon juice must be added last.

NOTE:

Recipe keeps in glass jar in the refrigerator for about 3 weeks. You can use this in the place of mayonnaise.

Feel 10 Times Better in One Week

7 DAYS OF DELIGHT	BREAKFAST	LUNCH	DINNER
SUNDAY	Sprouted Wheat Pancakes Apple Fruit Topping Fresh Fruit	General Tso's Tofu Whole Grain Brown Rice Broccoli Salad	Pizza Salad
MONDAY	Scrambled Tofu English Potatoes Bran Muffins Fresh Fruit	Ratatouille on Quinoa French Bread Salad	Split Pea Soup with Croutons Salad
TUESDAY	Breakfast Burritos Fresh Fruit	Vegetable Garden Soup Corn Bread Muffins Fresh Fruit or Salad	Cindy's Caprese Panino Sandwich Cream of Potato Soup
WEDNESDAY	Maple Banzo Waffles with Blueberry Fruit Topping Fresh Fruit	Spinach Tomato Quiche Steamed Kale Baked Acorn Squash Salad	Creamy Butternut Squash Soup with Gnocchi Salad
THURSDAY	Pancakes Raspberry Fruit Topping Fresh Fruit	Wheat Berry Meatballs Mixed Vegetables Rice or Potatoes Salad	Tostada Del Mundo
FRIDAY	Multigrain Goodness Cereal with Fresh and Dried Fruit and Maple Syrup	Manicotti Garlic Green Beans Salad Crusty Bread	Hearty Black Bean Soup Salad
SATURDAY	Breakfast Casserole Danish Pecan Rolls Fresh Fruit	Enchiladas Mexican Rice Hot Cheesy Mexican Dip Mexican Salsa Tortilla Chips	Veggie Burger sandwhiches with lettuce, tomato, onion, avacado, and Vegenaise; Mango/Banana Smoothie

More Family Reading

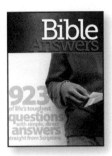

Bible Answers
You ask the questions; it points you to Bible texts with the answers

Lessons for Living
The true meaning hidden within the parables of Jesus

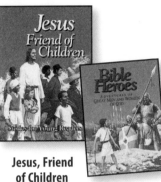

Jesus, Friend of Children
Favorite chapters from *The Bible Story*

Bible Heroes
A selection of the most exciting adventures from *The Bible Story*

The Story Book
Excerpts from Uncle Arthur's *Bedtime Stories*

My Friend Jesus
Stories for preschoolers from the life of Christ, with activity pages

Foods That Heal
A nutrition expert explains how to change your life by improving your diet

Plants That Heal
Unlocks the secrets of plants that heal the body and invigorate the mind

Seven Secrets Cookbook
Lose weight, lower cholesterol, reverse diabetes—healthy cuisine your family will love!

More Choices
All-natural meals you can make in 30 minutes

The Optimal Diet
The official CHIP cookbook, recipes to reverse and prevent lifestyle diseases

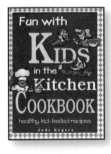

Fun With Kids in the Kitchen Cookbook
Let your kids help with these healthy recipes

Health Power
Choices you can make that will revolutionize your health

Joy in the Morning
Replace disappointment and despair with inner peace and lasting joy

FOR MORE INFORMATION:
- write
  Home Health Education Service
  P.O. Box 1119
  Hagerstown, MD 21741
- visit **www.thebiblestory.com**

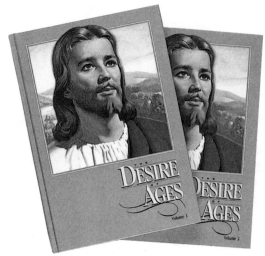

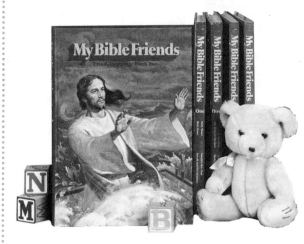